West Virginia Railroads
Volume 1: Railroading in the Mountain State
Thomas W. Dixon, Jr.

quarrier press

Charleston, West Virginia

ISBN 13: 978-1-942294-37-5
ISBN 10: 1-942294-37-9
Library of Congress Control Number: 2009940115

Formerly ISBN 0-939487-93-4

Layout and Design by
Karen Parker

Digital Reformatting by
Mark S. Phillips

Distributed by:

West Virginia Book Company
1125 Central Avenue
Charleston, West Virginia 25302
www.wvbookco.com

Title Page: A pair of B&O 2-8-8-0 pushers, numbers 7109 and 7202, are applying every ounce of their considerable tractive effort to the steel framed wagontop caboose, so characteristic of the B&O. The big mallets are helping an eastbound coal train, rounding the point of Salt Lick Curve west of Terra Alta, W. Va. at 11:26 AM on June 12, 1949. Note how the track bed is white from sand used for locomotive traction on the steep upgrade. Bruce D. Fales photo, Jay Williams Collection.

Table of Contents

Wheeling's 1952 Christmas season is in full swing, and the extra mail and express cars on Train 238 requires two locomotive — Class P-1d Pacifics 5085 and 5091 — for the two-hour romp to Pittsburgh. The ghostly crewman and baggage cart at right and the zigzagging beam of light from a car inspector's lantern at left are the result of a time exposure. J. J. Young photo, Bob Withers collection.

Foreword

The purpose of this book is to give the general reader an illustrated representative overview history of the railroads serving the state of West Virginia, accompanied by maps and photographs, with special concentration in the era from about 1940 into the 1960s. This was the period when steam locomotives were replaced by diesel-electrics and railroads faced strong competition from highways, airlines, and waterways, thus it is an era of change, evolving from the old standard of railroading into a new one. It is also one that is remembered with nostalgia by many people still living today (2009).

A complete and exhaustive history of railroading in West Virginia would be a huge undertaking and probably would have to be published in several volumes, since the state's history is so rich in the subject of railroads. It is my hope to follow this general overview treatment with a more detailed book on each of the major railroads which served West Virginia.

I have always believed that West Virginia, with its mountain railroading, logging lines, and mineral/forest product extraction history is every bit as interesting in railway history as Colorado. Much as been written about Colorado, with its narrow gauge lines likewise involved with mineral and lumber hauling, but West Virginia has not received nearly the same kind of treatment in books. This short introduction is intended to spur more interest in the state and its varied and interesting railroad operations.

My primary expertise is in the Chesapeake & Ohio Railway, but as a native West Virginian, and graduate of West Virginia University, I have always had an interest in the other railroads serving the state though I have had little chance to do any extensive research or collecting of data on them. Therefore, the preparation of this book has been a great learning experience, which I hope to expand as we develop follow-up books on some of the major West Virginia railroads, where we can further explore the interesting railroad operations within the state in much greater detail.

Although this book was prepared very quickly, I could not have accomplished it without the great work in design and layout by Karen Parker, who also gave excellent advice in other aspects of the book. Bob Withers helped immeasurably with the B&O chapter, and Lloyd D. Lewis edited and helped to write the Virginian and N&W chapters. In this first effort I have relied on photo collections that either I possess personally or which were readily available. Appreciation and acknowledgement is given to all those, living and dead, whose photos appear in these pages.

I expect that we will tap many other sources as we prepare the more detailed follow-up histories.

Thomas W. Dixon, Jr.
Lynchburg, Virginia
September 2009

Introduction

Since the era of the 1940s to the 1960s is the principal concentration of this book, its illustrative material was chosen to fit this period. This era was chosen because that is the period in which there is:

- First, a high degree of interest because it was a period of drastic transition. This transition was from steam to diesel motive power, but it was also the era when railroads began to lose their supremacy in transportation for most important commodities and for people. Although the transportation of coal remained, and still remains, almost exclusively with railroads, the passenger train suffered a steep decline after World War II, and eventually a tiny part of what remained was essentially nationalized under Amtrak in 1971. Coal transportation was and is the principal business of railroads in West Virginia, however its nature began a transition during this period as well.

- Second, the transportation of mail and express declined in concert with the passenger trains that hauled them, yet many people remember the passenger train from this time period when it mirrored many of the characteristics that had become so important in an earlier era.

- Third, the haulage of small, less-than-car-load shipments of freight, which was still the primary mode in 1945, it had been completely eliminated by motor freight by the early 1960s. This, coupled with the decline of the passenger service, changed the physical arrangement of railroads because staffed stations for freight and passenger business were no longer required at so many locations, since much of the business remaining shifted to large customers and bulk commodities.

- Fourth, the carriage of high value, time sensitive, through freight was eroded to a high degree by motor carriers. It is only in recent years that much of this traffic has returned to railroads in the form of trailers or containers being carried on flat

An N&W Y6 class 2-8-8-2 articulated has a mine shifter in southern West Virginia sometime in the late 1950s. (Gene Huddleston photo)

Mixed Train 458, pulled by Class B-18d Ten-Wheeler 2026, loafs down a steep 2.96 percent grade on Tuesday, Oct. 23, 1951, as it crosses a trestle just past Sandy Summit on its 33.2-mile trip from Spencer to Ravenswood. The middle-of-nowhere spot boasted one of the more spectacular pile trestles on the branch, and once railroad enthusiasts discovered it, they sometimes persuaded crews to carry them across, let them disembark in a cow pasture, back up, cross the span again for the benefit of their cameras, and pick them up again. (photo by Richard J. Cook, Allen County, Ohio, Historical Society Collection.)

cars. The traditional all purpose box cars of the earlier era have become a small element in today's railroading.

- Fifth, as patterns of traffic changed, the number of route miles of railroad main and branch lines decreased as many branches and unproductive main lines were abandoned and taken up in this era. This occurred especially in the decades following, as the railroads turned more to large shippers originating traffic at one point that was destined for one distant point. The coal business was particularly susceptible to this changing method of operation and shipment.

The conclusion is that railroads in general and in West Virginia in particular changed

how they operated almost completely – a change that was just beginning to occur in the 1940-1960 era of emphasis in the book. The railroads of 1945 were geared to their charter as "common carriers," providing transportation (of people, freight,

West Virginia Northern (a shortline connecting with the B&O) 2-8-0 #12 has a short train at Tunnelton, W. Va. in June, 1944. (TLC collection.)

In a scene that occurred as many as a dozen times a day, a C&O Allegheny type (2-6-6-6, class H-8) locomotive hauls a train of coal eastward toward tidewater at Tuckahoe, W.Va., just east of the state line with Virginia, which was located inside Alleghany tunnel, less than a mile in front of the locomotive. This particular photo was taken by the C&O company photographer in late 1942 to document the locomotive, which was brand new at the time. (C&O Railway photo, COHS Collection)

mail, and express) to the general public as well as to large bulk shippers. To do this many local stations and employees were needed.

Also to manage train operations in an era before highly sophisticated centralized signaling, more employees were needed to man towers located at frequent intervals to control switches and facilitate train movements. Steam locomotives were very hard on track structures and roadway, and as a result numerous maintenance of way employees were needed to keep the track in good condition.

At major division points (terminal yards located usually 60-80 miles apart where locomotives were serviced and train crews were changed and the cars in trains were often rearranged) roundhouses/engine houses with attached machine shops had to be maintained to do running repairs on locomotives. Steam locomotives tended to destroy themselves through the actions of heat and the throw weight of reciprocating parts, so they needed frequent detailed mechanical attention. Also there had to be facilities to supply water and

coal to them, which were consumed in prodigious quantities.

All this work required a large number of employees. Therefore, railroads were one of the largest employers within the state, only after coal mining and agriculture.

Along the line, stations were originally arranged so that a farmer could drive his horse-drawn vehicle to the station and return in a convenient time, so stations were positioned at frequent intervals at towns or sometimes in places where no large town was located. The average was probably five miles. This persisted into more modern times, but many of the smaller, rural stations began to be abandoned during this era after it had become much easier for people to travel longer distances by automobiles and trucks on improved roads.

The larger railroad systems of West Virginia (with the exception of the Virginian) had operations in many states and a variety of traffic and wide concerns, so their operations within the state were only part of a much larger operation. None had principal headquarters in the state except the Chesapeake & Ohio, which maintained it mechanical headquarters at Huntington along with a large staff from it coal department, and financial department.

In 1948 3,696 miles of railway were being operated by common carrier railroads in West Virginia (logging and industrial lines not included).

The principal large Class I system railroads operating in West Virginia were:

- Baltimore & Ohio operated in the eastern and northern panhandles and through the central and northern parts of the state on a generally east-west mainline direction but with a large number of branch lines principally serving the coal and lumber industries in the northern and central regions, and with important lines through the middle section of the state and along the western, Ohio River, border.

- Western Maryland entered the state near Ridgely, just across the Potomac from Cumberland, Maryland, and served coal and lumber business in the northeastern quadrant of the state in near proximity to B&O lines. Coal business flowed generally eastward to Baltimore.

- Chesapeake & Ohio operated in a generally east-west mainline direction through the southern part of the stated following the Greenbrier, New, and Kanawha Rivers and passing through Charleston and Huntington, with scores of branch lines for hauling coal from the New River, Kanawha, Coal River, Logan, and Greenbrier coal fields.

- Norfolk & Western also operated a generally east-west mainline entering the state near Bluefield and exiting at Kenova, and likewise had scores of coal branches in the rich Pocahontas coal fields in the extreme southern and western portion of the state.

- Virginian was a late comer to the state (completed 1909), and built with the overriding purpose of transporting West Virginia coal to piers at Norfolk to be loaded into coastwise and ocean-going ships. It had numerous coal mines in the general region also served by N&W and C&O and was always a competitor of both these lines. Unlike the latter two, its traffic was mainly eastbound.

- New York Central operated only a single line entering the state near Point Pleasant, running to Charleston and thence westward to Gauley Bridge and up Gauley to the Greenbrier coal fields. It was a comparatively minor player in the coal business, which mainly moved westward to its lines in Ohio. It operated lines jointly with C&O in the Greenbrier field (the Nicholas, Fayette & Greenbrier Railroad).

- The giant Pennsylvania Railroad had essentially no part in West Virginia railroading, however, a line running between Pittsburgh and Columbus did pass through the northern Panhandle, and a 50-mile branch extended from Wheeling to Chester, all in the Northern Panhandle, allowing PRR to serve the steel and heavy industry of Wheeling and Weirton. It also claimed a part in West Virginia coal fields production through its 1/3rd ownership in the Monongahela Railway (jointly owned with B&O and Pittsburgh & Lake Erie, itself a New York Central subsidiary)

- The Wheeling & Lake Erie and Pittsburgh & West Virginia railroads both alluded to the state in their names, but hardly touched it. W&LE was important as a connector from Wheeling, taking West Virginia coal and produce to the Midwest, but P&WV essentially just passed through a narrow neck of the Northern Panhandle.

The B&O opened the northern part of what is now West Virginia when it penetrated what was then northwestern Virginia before the War Between the States, but most of the rest of the area remained largely undeveloped or under-developed because no other railroads had built into its rugged landscape and dense forests. But, from the 1870s to the 1920s the state was alive with new railroad lines being built up hundreds of valleys, creeks, and rivers, as mining companies searched out coal–black diamonds–the fuel for the great American Industrial Revolution. The rich veins of bituminous or "soft" coal were among the best in the country to create steam for power or to use in steel making. Of course, it was only the coming of cheap and swift railroad transportation for huge amounts of the bulk shipment of coal that allowed this to occur. West Virginia and the railroads serving it had a large part in the creation of modern America and the modern industrial/technological world.

The other major railroad activity in the state

This caboose, photographed in about 1940, is the entire roster of equipment owned by the Kanwaha Central Railway, a 4.77-mile line that connected with C&O's Big Coal Subdivision at Brounland, West Virginia. It was a wholly-owned subsidiary of the Black Band Consolidated Coal Company of Olcott, W. Va., whose mine it served. C&O hopper cars are seen all around. (TLC Collection)

Lora Frazier's third-grade class boards Train 136 at Richwood in April 1954 for a ride down to their teacher's home a mile-and-a-half away for a near-the-end-of-the-school-year picnic. It looks like at least half of passenger/baggage combine 1452's 48 seats will be filled, at least for a few minutes, on this small segment of the train's 146-mile journey through the West Virginia hills from Richwood to Grafton. (Richwood News-Leader, Bob Withers collection.)

Western Maryland class H-7b Consolidation (2-8-0) #751 at Elkins, W.Va. The WM used Consolidations extensively for all kinds of service on the Elkins line and on branches, particularly on coal trains, were as many as five locomotives of this type were required to haul coal north to the WM main line. (TLC collection.)

was its logging railroads. To tap the huge virgin forests a way had to be forged to get the logs to the mills. The loggers used roughly built lines with specially designed locomotives and cars to accomplish this. From the mills the finished lumber was transported by the major railroads to markets all over the eastern United States. A great deal of the

housing in the eastern U. S. in the 1890s-1920s era was built with lumber from West Virginia forests. Coal always was the state's main resource, followed by forest products.

Because of its rough terrain and widely dispersed population, railroads remained the best

N&W electric #2511 at Bluefiled, W.Va. The N&W electrified the line over Elkhorn grade with locomotives of this type, relieving severe smoke problems caused by steam locomotives in the long Elkhorn Tunnel. The electrified section was removed when the N&W built a new, lower grade, line with a better ventilated tunnel in the early 1950s. (TLC collection.)

means of transportation for goods and people in West Virginia longer than in many other areas of the country, so the branch line passenger train and local freight held on here a little longer than in more developed and populated regions, and the railway era seemed to last into the space age.

Fortunately, the state has a number of tourist railroad operations and they are well publicized to the traveling public. This is helping to promote interest in the history of West Virginia railroading.

B&O 2-8-2 No. 4609 with an eastbound manifest train pauses at the foot of 17 Mile Grade at Piedmont, W. Va. to turn down the retainers on the train's air brakes on June 9, 1949. (Walter H. Thrall, Jr. photo, TLC Collection)

Whyte Wheel Arrangement Classification System

Steam Locomotives are classified by type based on their wheel arrangement. Locomotives have driving wheels which are used to change the power of the steam thrust on the cylinders into forward motion and pull. Guiding wheels in front of the drivers help guide it down the track and also support some of the front end weight. Wheels placed behind the drivers are always used to support the weight of the cab and firebox, and are always present when part or all of the firebox is located behind the last driver. The first element in the Whyte type represents the leading truck, the wheels out front, while the last represents the trailing wheels under the firebox and cab, while the number in between represents the driving wheels. On a rigid locomotive there are three numbers. For example an American type is a 4-4-0, meaning a four wheel leading (or engine) truck, four drivers, and no trailing wheels. A 2-8-2 means that there is a two wheel leading truck, eight drivers, and two wheels trailing under the firebox. With an articulated locomotive there can be several numbers between the leading and trailing trucks. For example a 2-8-8-2 means that there is a 2-wheel engine truck, a front engine with 8 drivers, and rear engine with 8 drivers, and a trailing truck with 2 wheels under the firebox, and so on.

A scene that could be found all through the coal fields of West Virginia: ranks of beehive coke ovens burning, converting coal to coke. Characteristic of such operations was the heavy pall of smoke blanketing the whole area. Miners' cottages can be seen on the hillside to the right. (TLC Collection.)

The Mallet

In Mallet's compound articulated design, two "engines" (a set of cylinders attached to a set of driving wheels is called an engine), were placed under a large boiler capable of a high volume of steam generation. The rear engine was attached to the frame and boiler rigidly as in any other locomotive, but the leading engine was set on a joint so that it could swivel freely around curves. This allowed the Mallet type to have the benefit of 12 or 16 driving wheels, but have only the rigid wheel base of 6 or 8, so it was highly adaptable to lines in the coal fields where curves were often sharp and branch lines that were laid with light rail and had light bridges, but where high power was needed to move heavy coal loads. The axle loads on the Mallet were lighter because of the weight distribution over so many wheels.

The second element of the design was that the boiler supplied high pressure steam to the rear set of cylinders. Once used to drive the rear set of wheels, this steam was piped by means of flexible joints to the front engine where it was used again at a much lower pressure before being exhausted up through the stack. This allowed the steam to do double duty, but it also required very large low-pressure cylinders, which were always set on the front so that they could be positioned in front of the boiler.

In the period up through the early 1920s, the Mallet was the preferred locomotive for use on slow heavy trains traveling over steep grades, a use that fit the coal haulers of West Virginia perfectly, and we find the Mallet extensively used by Virginian, N&W, C&O, B&O, and WM.

One of Virginian's Fairbanks Morse Trainmaster diesels with a loaded coal train near Mt. Hope in April, 1955. (Pat Dobbin photo, TLC Collection)

Mower Lumber rail truck No. 6 back in the woods sometime in the late 1940s or early '50s. We don't know what the purpose of the wooden rails that the truck is sitting on is, but they are certainly interesting. (TLC Collection)

N&W Y6b No. 2170 at Auville Yard, Yaeger, W. Va. in 1958. Note the diesel behind the locomotive, a portent of change. (Gene Huddleston photo)

B&O EL-5a 2-8-8-0 simple articulated with a train. This engine was originally built as a Mallet compound, and converted to simple operation by the railroad sometime between 1925 and 1930. The conversion was apparently successful, as the engine continued in service into the early 1950s. It is seen here at Terra Alta, W. Va. in June, 1944. (TLC Collection)

C&O G-7 class 2-8-0 No. 876 with a local passenger train at Glen Jean in July, 1948. Trains like this ran up every hollow in the first half of the 20th century, providing transportation in the era before paved roads and automobiles became common in the Mountain State. (COHS Collection)

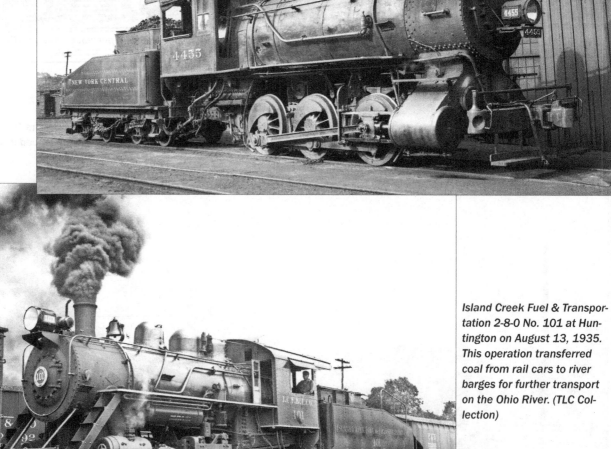

NYC 0-6-0 switcher No. 4455 at Charleston W. VA. on July 10, 1935. Switchers such as this were used to move cars to and from the heavy concentration of industry in the city. (TLC Collection)

Island Creek Fuel & Transportation 2-8-0 No. 101 at Huntington on August 13, 1935. This operation transferred coal from rail cars to river barges for further transport on the Ohio River. (TLC Collection)

Two westbound passenger trains are ready to depart Wheeling in December 1955. Class P7c Pacific No. 5318 simmers on No. 2 track with Pittsburgh-Louisville Train 233 and is due to leave at 10:45 a.m. Class P-6a Pacific No. 5231 heads up Wheeling-Kenova Train 73 on No. 3 track, and after receiving connecting mail, express and passengers, she will depart at 10:50 a.m. Both engineers will have had access to a bird's eye view northward along Wheeling's Market Street, as seen from the four-track viaduct just west of the Wheeling passenger station. (J.J. Young photo, Bob Withers Collection)

B&O Class P1d Pacific No. 5070 pulls westbound Train 233 down the middle of 17th Street in Wheeling just shy of the company's passenger station in December 1955. The four-car Pittsburgh-to-Louisville train, which carried a coach and coach/lunch counter car in addition to mail and express cars, was due to stop in Wheeling at 10:30 a.m. Later in the day, it also would call at Newark, Columbus and Cincinnati in Ohio. (J.J. Young photo, Bob Withers Collection)

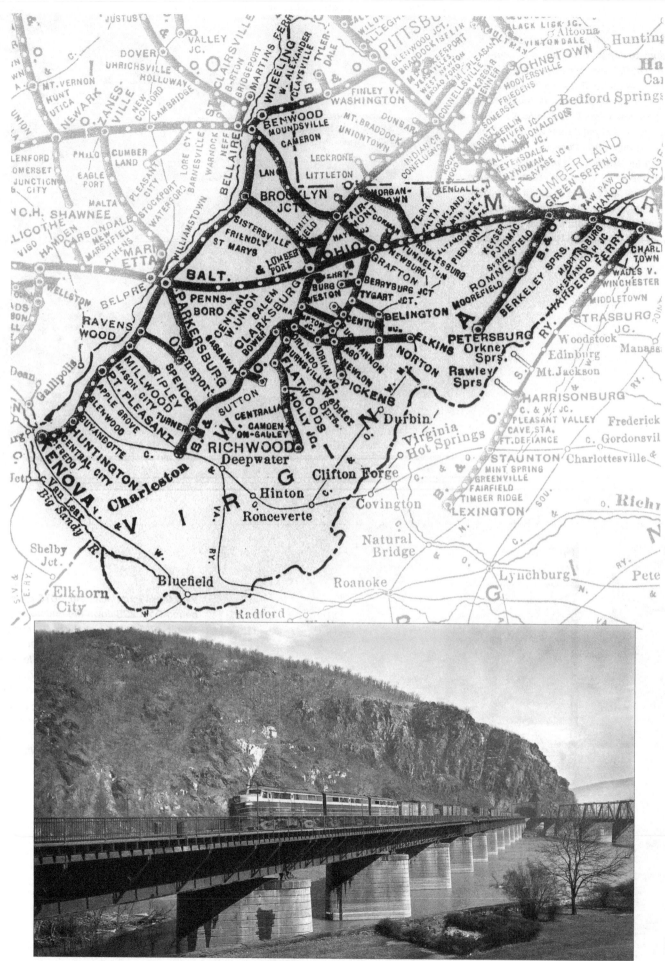

Baltimore and Ohio

The Baltimore & Ohio (B&O) was the first common carrier railroad to begin regular operations in the United States. Called the "mother of railroads," it was the standard against which other early lines measured themselves. As it built westward from its namesake city toward the Ohio River, it passed through the northern part of what was then the state of Virginia. This would later become West Virginia, and B&O's main line became important within the new state, especially after its expansion began in the era of coal and lumber extraction from the late 19th into the mid-20th Century. With the coming of large-scale coal mining in the fields of northern West Virginia near the B&O, the line became one of the state's four important coal haulers.

In 1825 the Erie Canal was opened, giving New York a decided advantage in facilitating trade between the frontier interior of the continent and navigation on the Atlantic Ocean, both up and down the coast of the U. S., and across the Ocean to Great Britain and Europe.

The following year the commonwealth of Pennsylvania began developing a canal system in response. In Maryland the Chesapeake & Ohio Canal was chartered in 1824 to connect Washington with the "Western Waters," but Baltimore was left without a project to compete with these moves and to promote its commerce with the interior.

However, at about this time railroad technology burst forth, first in Great Britain, but soon in America as well, resulting in the charter of the B&O on February 28, 1827. The first stone of the B&O was laid with great ceremony on July 4, 1828 with Charles Carroll, the last surviving signer of the Declaration of Independence, among the participants.

B&O's main line left Baltimore along the Patapsco River, followed the route of the Monocacy River to the Potomac, and westward along that important waterway. In 1834 the line reached the Maryland side of the Potomac opposite Harper's Ferry. A bridge to the (W.) Virginia side was opened in 1837. There it connected with the Winchester & Potomac Railroad, building up the Shenandoah Valley from Winchester to Harper's Ferry (which line later became a part of the B&O system).

From Harper's Ferry the B&O line was pushed westward to Cumberland, Maryland, already an important city on the Chesapeake & Ohio Canal. Ultimately, Cumberland would be one of the most important operational and mechanical centers on the B&O. The former B&O locomotive shops at Cumberland remain today as one of the principal locomotive repair facilities on the giant CSX system. It was situated just across the Potomac from (West) Virginia. After skirting the (West) Virginia/Maryland border westward, the B&O main line veered southwestward to the town of Grafton, where it then turned northwest toward the Ohio River city of Wheeling, to fulfill its charter and meet the great commercial traffic then building up via the Ohio River and its connections with the Mississippi and other rivers of what was then called the "Great West."

Wheeling was reached in 1852, and the line was officially opened January 1, 1853. To obtain a more direct rail route to Cincinnati and St. Louis, in 1851 B&O incorporated another line as the Northwestern Virginia Railroad that was built almost due west 101 miles from Grafton to Parkersburg on the Ohio. It was opened on May 1, 1857. Parkersburg lay directly across the Ohio from Marietta, where The Marietta and Cincinnati Railroad was built to meet the B&O. To inaugurate through service on June 1, 1857, B&O ran a special train over these lines, reaching Cincinnati two days later, and on to St. Louis the following day via the Ohio & Mississippi Railroad, which completed a through route broken only by a ferry transfer across the Ohio at Parkersburg. The Marietta & Cincinnati and Ohio & Mississippi both became integral parts of the B&O's through line and were eventually merged.

Opposite: The B&O mainline from the East first enters West Virginia as it crosses the Potomac River into the town of Harpers Ferry. This view from the town side shows a beautiful set of B&O FA model Alco diesels with a long freight train about to enter West Virginia, which was taken in the early 1950s. Maryland Heights is on the hill in the background. - (TLC Collection)

Early in its career, the B&O began to haul coal from West Virginia. In 1853 it hauled 309,890 tons east from Cumberland, despite strong competition from the Chesapeake & Ohio Canal, proving at an early date that railroads were far superior to canals for carrying large quantities of heavy materials long distances cheaply. By 1955, at the height of the post-WWII coal boom, B&O carried 48,500,000 tons of bituminous coal, over half of which came from West Virginia mines.

The War Between the States forestalled further B&O expansion for almost a decade. John Brown's raid occurred at Harper's Ferry, right on the B&O main line, and throughout the war B&O was an important link for transferring the Federal armies and supplies moving east-west. Hostilities resulted in considerable destruction to portions of the line on several occasions. In one famous incident Stonewall Jackson raided the B&O at Martinsburg and sized a number of locomotives, which he then transported down the Shenandoah Valley by highway to Winchester.

Control of the Marietta & Cincinnati and Ohio & Mississippi lines was strengthened and bridges were built across the Ohio at Wheeling in 1868 and Parkersburg in 1871. In 1867 B&O leased the Central Ohio Railroad operating between Bellaire, Ohio (across the river from Wheeling), and continued its westward expansion from that point. Other lines through Ohio reached Akron, Columbus, Cleveland, Toledo, and across Indiana to Chicago as well as a line from Cincinnati to Springfield and through Illinois. A line to Pittsburgh and west connected with other lines, giving B&O basically two important through passenger routes: Washington to Chicago via Pittsburgh, and Washington to St. Louis via Parkersburg and Cincinnati.

B&O was important in a famous labor strike that occurred at Martinsburg shops in 1877 as part of a nationwide railroad strike of epic proportions. The strike that began at this point spread across American railroads and resulted in a huge conflict involving the use of Federal troops to keep order.

Class EM-1 2-8-8-4 simple articulated takes loaded coal train east around Salt Lick Curve near Terra Alta circa 1950. (Railroad Avenue Enterprises Collection)

By 1900 B&O was an important trunk line for through freight and passengers, and was developing the coal fields in northern West Virginia through a series of branch lines radiating from Fairmont and Grafton. It purchased the Coal & Coke Railroad, running from Elkins down through the central part of the state to Charleston. The Coal & Coke was completed in 1905 under the leadership of Henry Gassaway Davis after acquisition of the Charleston, Clendenin & Southern and other proposed and actual lines. Its principal connection was with the West Virginia Central & Pittsburg [sic] (later Western Maryland) at Elkins and with B&O near Burnsville. At Charleston, the Coal & Coke connected with the New York Central's Kanawha & Michigan, and indirectly with the Chesapeake & Ohio. Its territory was rich in lumber, coal, and petroleum (after 1912). The line's principal terminal and yard was at Gassaway, about halfway along the line. B&O took control of the road in 1917 and it remained a part of that system until abandonment of most of its line in the 1970s.

The C&C was never a large originator of traffic although the line had considerable business in petroleum and petroleum products when B&O acquired it. It proved very useful in connecting the B&O with Charleston and with numerous coal properties along the way. Eventually it became important as a coal originator as well.

The Ohio River Railroad, extending along the West Virginia bank of that river from Wheeling through Parkersburg to Huntington and Kenova was originally built in the early 1880s and became part of the B&O system in 1901. B&O was attempting to break into the coal fields of eastern Kentucky and the Ohio River line would serve as its access, however this never occurred since C&O had the lead in that area and B&O was never able to overcome its control of the region. The Ohio

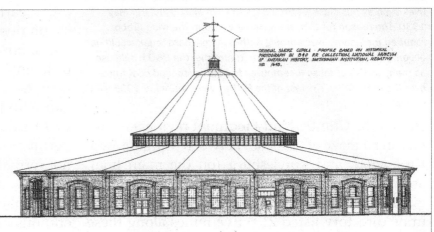

Martinsburg was the first important B&O operational point in West Virginia. Located in the Eastern Panhandle of the state, just 18 miles west of Harpers Ferry, it became an important yard and shop point before the War Between the States. Two fully enclosed roundhouses were built here, and lasted into modern times. This drawing was made by the Historic American Engineering Record to record the unique building that survived. Almost all roundhouses built after the 1860s were open in the center, even if they were complete circles. (Historic American Engineering Record Photo and Drawing)

River line is today still an important link in CSX's West Virginia operations between Huntington, Parkersburg, and Wheeling.

During the decades from 1890 through 1920, B&O acquired most of its coal-producing branches and gained its place as one of the four large haulers of West Virginia-originated bituminous coal (along with C&O, N&W and Virginian). Coal and coke (much of it from the West Virginia fields) accounted for about 60% of the B&O's freight traffic by this time.

B&O's principal coal lines in West Virginia in-

B&O was one of the railroads known for its "Camelback" locomotives such as this class E-19a 2-8-0 shown in Martinsburg in May 1930. The reason for the arrangement was that the wide firebox, required for locomotives burning Anthracite or "hard" coal, would not accommodate the cab at the rear. In their time, the B&O would use as many as five of these locomotives to haul eastbound coal trains over the mountains. The last of the E-19as were retired in 1935 (TLC Collection)

cluded the Cumberland-Piedmont region, encompassing a maze of branches between Morgantown, Kingwood, and Rowlesburg (on the main line), and along the mainline, as well as the West Virginia Northern shortline feeder. B&O's 1937 coal mine directory listed 21 active mines along these lines in West Virginia.

The "West Virginia Coal Region," as B&O termed it in 1937, encompassed branches in Upshur, Barbour, Taylor, Harrison, and Marion counties with the principal marshalling yard and terminal at Fairmont. Sixty-five active mines were shown in the 1937 directory. An additional 31 mines were listed on the Monongahela Railroad in this region. The Monongahela was a short line controlled jointly by the B&O, Pennsylvania, and Wheeling & Lake Erie (which was a NYC subsidiary) railroads for the exploitation of coal in both West Virginia and Pennsylvania.

In the central portion of the state another B&O coal region was the "Roaring Creek, Upshur, Belington, Gauley, and Clay-Elk Coal District." This comprised 33 mines operating along branches primarily along the old Coal & Coke Railroad's mainline in Upshur, Randolph, Gilmer, Braxton, Webster, Clay, and Nicholas counties. A few operations were also shown south of Wheeling in Ohio

and Marshall counties.

B&O's main operating points in West Virginia remained Grafton and Fairmont in the coal regions, as well as the already-mentioned terminals at Martinsburg, Parkersburg, Wheeling (Benwood), and Gassaway.

The B&O continued as an important national, regional, and West Virginia coal hauler through World Wars I and II, but after the second war its operations were burdened by a large debt and declining coal volume.

An early proponent of diesels, B&O continued steam operations through the later 1950s in some areas, but by that time it was unable to upgrade or maintain its lines or equipment in an adequate way. As a result, starting in 1958, discussions began with the highly profitable C&O for a merger. C&O acquired B&O stock, eventually gaining ICC permission to control the B&O in 1963. Although not formally merged, the two roads gradually began to combine management and transportation, maintenance, mechanical, and engineering operations in the decade following, under the name "C&O/B&O Railroads." Western Maryland was controlled, but it continued independent operations. Finally, in 1972 C&O and B&O (followed by WM in 1975) began a completely unified operation under the holding company Chessie System Railroads.

Soon after C&O took control, B&O closed its 80-mile line between Clarksburg and Parkersburg while it undertook a large project to increase clearances and thus permit haulage of piggyback trailers and autorack cars. The $8.5 million job, part of a system-wide improvement plan funded with C&O money, involved lowering the floors of five tunnels, enlarging four more, bypassing three, and replacing one with a new bore on a different alignment.

Passenger and freight trains were detoured via Brooklyn Junction (New Martinsville) on the Ohio River and Short Line subdivisions during the closure, which lasted from May 13 to October 27 – longer than planned. Trains 1 and 2, the *National*

22

Limited, and Trains 11 and 12, the *Metropolitan Special*, were detoured, but buses were substituted for Cumberland-to-Cincinnati Trains 23 and 30 between the affected points.

Ironically, the improvements – which boosted freight traffic by 20 percent almost immediately after the line was reopened – proved to be the beginning of the end for the route. Train No. 2's St. Louis-Washington coach and sleeping car, and the San Antonio-St. Louis-Washington Slumbercoach had been diverted to C&O's *George Washington* at Cincinnati during the project, serving to convince B&O it could do without its own line between Parkersburg and Clarksburg.

Two years later, the *National Limited's* through cars were diverted to C&O in both directions. After Amtrak's takeover of passenger trains, it operated the *Shenandoah* between Washington and Cincinnati over the B&O's Cumberland-Grafton-Parkersburg-Cincinnati line between 1976 and 1981, which was the last passenger train on the line.

The line was finally closed for good and freight traffic diverted after an excursion was operated between Grafton and Parkersburg on September 15, 1985. Thus, one of the biggest and most expensive modernization projects undertaken by any West Virginia railroad was abandoned only a few years after its completion.

In 1981, Chessie System was consolidated with Seaboard System (itself a combination of the old Atlantic Coast Line, Seaboard Air Line, Louisville & Nashville, Clinchfield, Georgia Railroad, and others) into CSX Transportation. CSX today operates much of the trackage in West Virginia originally part of B&O, C&O, and WM. The B&O line from Grafton to Buckhannon, Burnsville, and Cowan is leased from CSX by a short line operator, the Paducah & Louisville Railroad.

A portion of the old Coal & Coke line from Burnsville to Gassaway is owned by short line Elk River Railroad but as of this writing is not in operation. It is also in possession of the former BC&G

In the valley behind this Monongahela light 2-8-2 is the Monongahela River at Fairmont, W. Va. No. 172 (class L-1) was one of ten USRAs built by Alco in 1919. It is replete with interesting variations of detail not on the locomotive as built. By July, 1939, the date of this photo, a Delta trailing truck had been added, a ladder attached to the Walschaerts valve gear hanger, perforations on the front ladders, spoked pilot truck wheels, a trailing truck booster, and a modified tender, with increased coal and water space. (M.D. McCarter Collection).

The Monongahela Railway was an independent operation that provided coal to B&O through connections in the latter's northern West Virginia coal region. Mines on this line originated coal that was delivered to B&O at Rivesville in West Virginia and Leckrone, Pennsylvania. Most Monongahela lines were in Pennsylvania, but several were south of the West Virginia border. It was jointly owned by the Pittsburgh & Lake Erie (thus NYC), Pennsylvania Railroad (and was the PRR's only activity in the West Virginia coal region) and the B&O, each line having a 1/3rd interest after 1927. The Monongahela ran its last passenger trains in 1950 and dieselized between 1952 and 1954. The company ceased independent operation in 1993, merging into Conrail.

short line (see page 114)

The original B&O mainline through Grafton and Wheeling remains in operation, as well as the Ohio River line. The former B&O line from Tygart to Belington and Elkins in operated primarily as a tourist excursion line by a short line operator.

Sir John's Run, W. Va., was 28.7 miles west of Martinsburg, and because of the triple track and photogenic terrain, many official B&O company photos were taken here. This one shows a massive 2-8-8-4 EM-1 simple articulated at left, while a set of three model FT diesels occupies the center track and a blurred freight heads in the other direction. This was in the height of the steam-diesel transition on the B&O in the late 1940s. (B&O Photo, TLC Collection)

Two EM-1 simple 2-8-8-4s were serious power, but here they are on a freight on the Magnolia Cutoff which led the B&O main line around the original, twisting line. This scene is at Paw Paw, W. Va. - From the point where the original B&O mainline entered West Virginia at Harper's Ferry until it reached a point east of Terra Alta, it passed across the W. Va./Md. Border seven times as it roughly followed the Potomac River. (Bruce Fales Photo, Jay Williams Collection)

EM-1 class 2-8-8-4 simple articulated, B&O's only class of modern "Super Power" steam, pauses here at Piedmont, W. Va. at the foot of 17-mile grade while an S-1 class 2-10-2 Santa Fe type eases up beside it, ready to couple on the front and help it up the steep grade. (Railroad Ave. Enterprises Collection)

The West Virginia/Maryland border marker is prominent in this photo of B&O F7 diesels hauling all Mail & Express Train No. 29 approaching Keyser. About eight miles west of here the line jogged into Maryland for a short space, then back to W. Va., then back across the line, for a trip across the western extremity of that state and into West Virginia for good, east of Terra Alta. (Bill Price Photo)

EM-1 class 2-8-8-4 simple articulated, B&O's only class of modern "Super Power" steam, pauses here at Piedmont, W. Va. at the foot of 17-mile grade while an S-1 class 2-10-2 Santa Fe type eases up beside it, ready to couple on the front and help it up the steep grade. (Railroad Ave. Enterprises Collection)

This hazy, smoky scene was the way it looked at M&K Junction in 1947 as steam still ruled much of the B&O's mainline traffic across the mountains out of West Virginia. The cinder conveyor at left has just dumped ashes into the waiting hoppers as the big locomotives at right take their turn to have their fires cleaned over the ash pit. (TLC Collection).

0-8-8-0 Mallet No. 7032 is seen here pushing hard out of M&K Junction with an east-bound fast freight train May 15, 1940. B&O had a number of articulated locomotives without leading or trailing trucks. They were employed almost exclusively as pushers, where the absence of the leading truck was not a problem. (Bruce Fales Photo, Jay Williams Collection)

A superb night photo shows Mikado No. 4407 at M&K Junction on September 28, 1948. M&K Junction was the point as which the Morgantown & Kingwood line joined the mainline about 26 miles east of Grafton. An engine servicing facility was maintained here to accommodate the pusher locomotives that were dispatched to handle trains going west on the Cheat Grade and east on the Cranberry Grade. (Bruce Fales Photo, Jay Williams Collection)

In another panoramic view of the famous Salt Lick curve of Cranberry Grade west of Terra Alta, four F-unit diesels power a long coal train. We can't see the helpers on the rear, but they're likely steam in this early 1950s steam-diesel transition era photo. (TLC Collection)

Twin portals of Kingwood Tunnel were near the aptly named town of Tunnelton. The right bore has its ashlar stone portal and the newer one at left has a concrete portal. The first Kingwood Tunnel was built in 1852 during B&O's push westward and was a target of Confederate raiders in 1863. Always a bottleneck, the second bore was completed in 1912. B&O Mail & Express Train No. 29 is bursting out of the west end of the tunnel with two Pacific types and 22 cars in October 1947. (TLC Collection)

This excellent scene shows a troop train leaving Grafton terminal in May 1953, with Pacific (4-6-2) type No. 5068 for power. The large impressive station is barely visible at left, and the towering Second Empire style Willard Hotel is prominent to the left background. The large concrete coaling station dominated the yard overall. Grafton was a key location for B&O in operating its main line trains as well as the coal trains that came out of the many branches to its south and west. (Phillip R. Hastings Photo, Bob Withers Collection)

B&O 2-8-8-0 EL-3a Class No. 7132 rests at Grafton engine terminal September 14, 1937. A sharp eye will identify this as a "simple" articulated, meaning that high pressure steam was used in all cylinders. This is also indicated by the two stacks, for exhausts from each of the cylinders sets. Built by Baldwin Locomotive Works as a Mallet compound in 1917, B&O later rebuilt it as a simple locomotive to add power. Grafton was the major locomotive terminal for B&O's West Virginia operations, both main and branch lines. (Jay Williams Collection)

Often-photographed daylight Mail & Express Train No. 29 is seen leaving Grafton with an F7AB set in October 1954, as Mikado (2-8-2) 4412 and 0-8-0 switcher 620, both probably having recently been removed from service as B&O steadily dieselized in this period. With a peak population of 8,500 in 1920, Grafton was very similar to Hinton on the C&O far to the south, with its coal operations and through mainline service. As Hinton was tied directly to C&O, so Grafton's life was tied directly to B&O. (Howard Barr, Sr. Photo)

B&O's streamlined Pacific No. 5303 with The Cincinattian coasts across the Tygart Valley River bridge toward its daily station stop at Grafton in 1947 during the three years when the five-car streamliner operated between Baltimore-Washington and Cincinnati. Ultimately a failure on this route, it was moved to a Cincinnati-Detroit run in 1950. But for a while its daylight run across the B&O in West Virginia gave passengers a view of spectacular mountain scenery. (Bruce Fales Photo, Jay Williams Collection)

Opposite Top: Clarksburg was an important town on the B&O mainline west of Grafton which handled a large amount of mail for the northern West Virginia region, and was a center of the coal fields. Calling at the neat brick station with its platform canopy at left is Mail/Express No. 29 on August 8, 1951. (E. L. Thompson Photo, B&O RR Historical Society Collection)

Opposite Center: Mail/Express Train No. 29 is again seen here, leaving West Virginia westbound on the approach to the Ohio River bridge on September 26, 1951. (E. L. Thompson Photo, B&O RR Historical Society Collection)

Opposite Bottom: B&O gas-electric car No. 6044 with a trailing car for mail and express has just arrived at Parkersburg's 6th Street Station after its short trip from Zanesville, Ohio, as Train No. 56 on September 20, 1945. Like many railroads, B&O handled some of its local and branch line business with motor cars rather than steam-powered trains. (John F. Humiston Photo)

Baltimore and Ohio R. R. Depot and Train Shed, Wheeling. W. Va.

B&O's original main line fulfilled the "Ohio" of its name when it reached Wheeling in what was then Virginia in 1853. When the "Restored Government of Virginia" broke away from the Old Dominion it set up its capital at Wheeling, and then Wheeling became the first capital of new West Virginia in 1863. Important as a river trading town it developed an important steel and heavy industrial base. B&O's huge Second Empire style station was pride of the city when this postcard was printed about 1915. (TLC Collection)

Right: B&O train No. 33 with one of the line's classic Pacific types is seen here leaving Wheeling station for Cincinnati, in May 1956, having come in from Pittsburgh. Its trip through West Virginia territory was just across the narrow Northern Panhandle. Though Wheeling may be one the best known cities in West Virginia, many think it's much more akin to western Pennsylvania. (J. J. Young, Jr. photo, Bob Withers Collection)

Pounding through a driving snow storm, B&O Train No. 430 handled by P-4 class Pacific No. 5137 passes the Wheeling Steel plant at Benwood, in December 1950. (J. J. Young, Jr. photo, Bob Withers Collection)

In July 1956 a number of B&O steam locomotives were stored dead at Benwood Junction, while others were very much active. Benwood Junction was a yard, engine terminal, and servicing point located about six miles south of Wheeling that was the principal operating point for the B&O lines converging on Wheeling. (Joe Schmitz Photo)

B&O Pacific No. 5231 pauses at the stylish brick Moundsville station on its run with Train No. 73, operating Pittsburgh, Wheeling, Parkersburg, Huntington and terminating at Kenova. This 233-mile run skirted the Ohio River on its West Virginia side all the way. Moundsville is located about 11 miles south of Wheeling and was named for the American Indian burial mounds prevalent in the area. (J. J. Young, Jr. Photo, Bob Withers Collection)

B&O passenger trains from Wheeling and Parkersburg ended their runs along the West Virginia side of the Ohio River at Huntington and Kenova. Here B&O Pacific No. 5220 has a two-car train at the B&O Huntington depot in May 1956. The station is now used as a visitor's center and restaurant, with other stores located nearby in the former freight station. (H. H. Harwood, Jr. Photo)

B&O Mikado (2-8-2) No. 4564 is at the engine terminal in Charleston on a hot July day in 1956, ready for northbound work on the old Coal & Coke line up through the center of the state after taking on fuel from the direct coaling machine seen in the background. This simple machine took coal from a pit under a hopper car and conveyed it into the tender, in a much simpler operation than the huge overhead coaling station tower. (Joe Schmitz Photo)

On the branch running south from Grafton into the coal fields is the town of Buckhannon. At that point we see one of B&O's ubiquitous Q-class 2-8-2s (a Q-3 in this case) with a caboose about ready to handle a mine run or local freight seen in the background in July 1956. (Jim Shaughnessy photo, Bob Withers Collection)

The engineer "oils around" with his traditional long-spouted oil can as B&O 2-8-2 Mikado No. 4592 takes on coal at Buckhannon July 1, 1956. At smaller terminals such as this B&O used "automatic coaling machines." This device consisted of a permanently installed conveyor leading from a pit to the tender. A hopper of coal was positioned over the pit and the coal was conveyed to the tender as it fell into the pit from the hopper car. (Jim Shaughnessy photo, Bob Withers Collection)

Representative of large-scale coal mines on the B&O is this tipple at Norton, which was used in an advertisement in the 1937 B&O coal mine directory B&O Coals. It was certainly a very modern facility by the standards of that time. Norton is located on B&O's line between Elkins and Tygart Junction. (TLC Collection)

Coal performance is dependent upon fool-proof preparation and inherent high quality.

Steam...By-product ...Gas...Metallurgical...Ceramic and Domestic.

20,000 TONS DAILY CAPACITY

NORTON STEAM AND DOMESTIC

MEDIUM LOW-VOLATILE COAL—Mined at Norton, W. Va., on the BALTIMORE & OHIO RAILROAD.

This is typical of a very small tipple, loading run-of-the-mine coal at the Henshaw Mine at Brownton, W. Va. on B&O's Astor Branch in the Fairmont Field. Although most B&O coal came from large, mechanized tipples, some small operations such as this were always present until the more modern era. (From 1937 B&O Coal Mine Directory, TLC Collection)

The Three Fork Coal Company operated this four track tipple at its mine on the Middle Fork Railroad, a short line operated for extraction of the coal as well as the Moore, Keppel Company's logging operations. Cars were hauled down the 13-mile line from Cassity to the end of the B&O branch at Midvale. (From 1937 B&O Coal Mine Directory)

This series of three photos taken from the 1937 B&O Coals shows the preparation of coal at the tipple. The first shows men handling very large lump coal on a sorting table at the Mobley Mine Tipple at Elm Grove, W. Va. – The second shows 6-inch lump coal loaded at Koppers Coal Company, at Grant Town, W. Va. – The third shows 1-inch stove coal neatly falling into hoppers at the Three Fork Coal Company mine at Cassity, W. Va.

This interesting advertisement by Jones Collieries appeared in the 1937 B&O Coals and showed an artist's rendering of the very modern looking Rachel Mine tipple, located near Mannington in B&O's Fairmont coal fields.

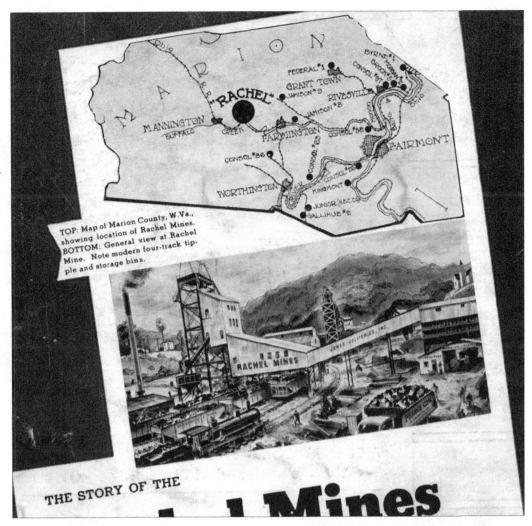

TOP: Map of Marion County, W.Va., showing location of Rachel Mines. BOTTOM: General view at Rachel Mine. Note modern four-track tipple and storage bins.

THE STORY OF THE

A classic scene of rural railroading in West Virginia is this view mixed Train 458 (both passenger and freight) hauled by B&O 4-6-0 Ten-Wheeler No. 2026 near Sandy Summit on June 26, 1952. Its passengers as well as any mail or express for the Ravenswood, Spencer & Glenville Branch were handled in the combination car. The train left Spencer at 10:50 am, arriving at Ravenswood (34 miles) in time to connect with a train to Parkersburg and points north, then returned to Spencer after the arrival at Ravenswood of the southbound train from Wheeling and Parkersburg. There were 20 flag stops listed in between, averaging 1-1/3 mile apart! A timetable from 1950 for this train and its eastbound counterpart is shown. (Richard J. Cook Photo, Bob Withers Collection)

73-457	Mls.	April 30, 1950.	458-72	
		(Eastern time.)		
		(Ann Street Station.)		
*1 55 P M	0	lve..+Parkersburg....arr.	*2 55 P M	
*2 53 P M	34.6	arr....Ravenswood....lve.	*1 58 P M	
†3 10 P M	0	lve..+Ravenswood....arr.	†1 10 P M	
– –	0.5	...R. S. & G. Junction...	– –	
f3 24 "	3.2	.........Silverton	f1250 "	
f3 31 "	4.9	.........Varners.........	f12 41 "	
f3 35 "	6.3	....Crow Summit.......	f1237 "	
f3 40 "	7.9	.........New Era.........	f1230 "	
f3 42 "	8.3	.........Sandyville.......	12 25 "	
f3 47 "	10.0	.........Murray.........	f12 16 "	
f3 57 "	12.6	.... Meadowdale........	f1208 P M	
f4 01 "	14.4	.... Duncan..........	f1200 Noon	
f4 06 "	15.8	.... Leroy..........	f1155 A M	
f4 11 "	17.0	.... Liverpool........	11 52 "	
f4 19 "	18.8	......Sandy Summit......	f1145 "	
f4 22 "	19.9	........Sun Flower........	f1135 "	
f4 25 "	21.0	.... Seaman	f1130 "	
f4 27 "	21.6	.... Dukes	f1128 "	
f4 38 "	23.1	.... Reedy..........	11 25 "	
f4 43 "	24.9	.... Moores........	f1115 "	
f4 54 "	27.1	.........Billings.........	f1110 "	
f4 59 "	29.1	..........Depue..........	f1100 "	
f5 03 "	30.0	...........Barrs...........	f1057 "	
f5 08 "	31.8	...... Nancy Run.......	f1053 "	
†5 25 P M	33.1	.... Spencer	†1050 A M	
		....ARRIVE] [LEAVE....		

A westbound B&O passenger train crosses the Potomac River from Maryland into Harpers Ferry, W.Va. We do not know the date, but the streamliner appears to be the Chicago-bound Capitol Limited, which was modernized in 1938. The EA diesels were built in 1937 and lasted on the property until 1953. (B&O Photo, TLC Collection)

B&O Train No. 4, The Diplomat, with 2-8-2s Nos. 4416 and 4405 and E-7A and B (No. 64 leading) with 12 cars on Salt Lick Curve, Terra Alta, August 17, 1947. (E.L. Thompson photo, B&O RR Historical Society collection)

A pair of B&O 2-8-8-0 pushers, numbers 7109 and 7202, are applying every ounce of their considerable tractive effort to the steel framed wagontop caboose, so characteristic of the B&O. The big mallets are helping an eastbound coal train, rounding the point of Salt Lick Curve west of Terra Alta, W. Va. at 11:26 AM on June 12, 1949. Note how the track bed is white from sand used for locomotive traction on the steep upgrade. (Bruce D. Fales photo, Jay Williams Collection.)

B&O Train No. 30 with engines 4409 and 4449, both 2-8-2s, with 7 cars, west of Terra Alta on July 22, 1951. (TLC Collection)

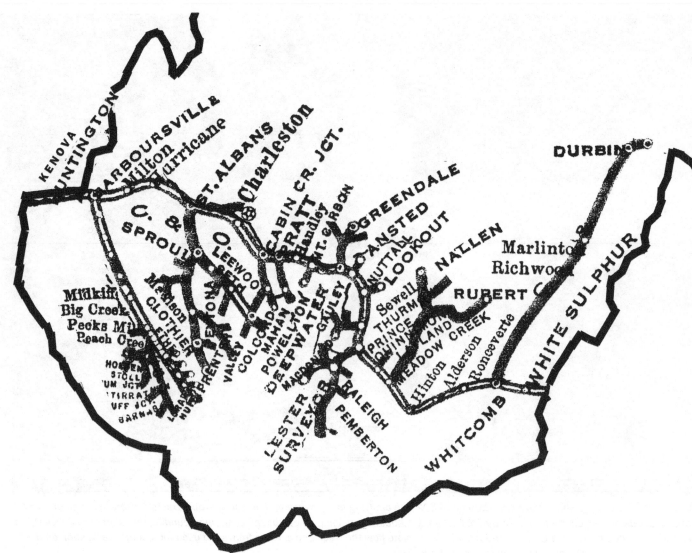

Chesapeake and Ohio

The Chesapeake & Ohio (C&O) traces its lineal descent from the Louisa Railroad, chartered in 1836 to build a line in Louisa County, Virginia, to take farm products to market. The line was successful, and expanded so that by 1850 it had reached Richmond to the southeast and Charlottesville to the northwest of its original line, With its designs on further expansion, the name was changed to Virginia Central in that year.

By 1854 the line had pushed across the Blue Ridge (with help from the Commonwealth of Virginia through the state-financed Blue Ridge Railroad) and Shenandoah ranges and had reached the foot of the Alleghany range. Meanwhile the Virginia General Assembly had also incorporated another state-backed line to build on to the Ohio River from the Virginia Central's endpoint at Covington, under the name Covington & Ohio Railroad. Work was commenced, but soon halted because of the War Between the States. After the war and West Virginia's statehood, the Virginia Central and the Covington & Ohio (the later contained almost wholly within the new state), were combined under the new name Chesapeake & Ohio. The C&O was able to attract financial backing by Collis P. Huntington, who was at the time (1869) just finishing his work on the Central Pacific portion of the Transcontinental Railroad. His idea was to use C&O as an eastern link to a "true transcontinental" under the control of one company or person (him).

In the summer of 1869 the C&O built across Alleghany (spelled with an "a" in this region) summit and reached White Sulphur Springs, West Virginia, which had been an important destination for passengers since the stage-coach days of the 1820s. From then onward White Sulphur Springs

Opposite: An eastbound heavy coal train of 125 cars (about 7,000 tons) is climbing the Alleghany grade at Tuckahoe, W. Va., with a giant 2-6-6-6 type locomotive, the most powerful locomotive ever to operate on C&O and among the biggest of all time. The year is 1942 and the H-8 is brand new. About ½-mile in front of the train is Alleghany Tunnel where the C&O mainline crosses the Virginia-West Virginia border. C&O had the best grade (half-a foot rise to 100 feet of travel) of any of the roads taking West Virginia coal eastward. NOTE: In this part of the Virginias Alleghany is spelled with an "a." (C&O Ry. photo, C&OHS Collection)

would be an important factor in C&O passenger service, and in later days, passengers were brought in from the great northeastern cities so that they could "take the waters," in the European spa style. As late as the 1960s passenger traffic, particularly from the Northeastern cities, to White Sulphur Springs' Greenbrier Hotel (owned by C&O after 1910) was a very important element in C&O's passenger operations (see below).

From 1869 through the spring of 1873 C&O's line was built across the state, reaching the Ohio River at the new city of Huntington, established by and named for C. P. Huntington. In the 1870s C&O began shipping coal eastward to Richmond and points east, and set a pattern that it would follow down to the present day. Because it had no good railroad connection at Huntington, its traffic on to Cincinnati was by steamboat. By 1881 a connection via Huntington controlled railroads in Kentucky helped it reach Louisville and also Cincinnati in a round-about way. Finally, in 1888 the line down the south (Kentucky) side of the river was built and an impressive bridge took C&O into the Queen City.

Huntington held control of the C&O throughout this period and for a couple of years actually achieved his true transcontinental with C&O as its eastern link, but he soon lost the C&O, which fell into hands of the Vanderbilts. Under its new leadership C&O was completely rebuilt and upgraded through the 1890s, at the very time that coal was becoming its most important traffic. It also started up an important and highly advertised through passenger service. Its trains originated in New York and traveled over the Pennsylvania Railroad to Washington, over the predecessor of the Southern Railway to Charlottesville and thence over the C&O through Virginia, West Virginia, and Kentucky, to Cincinnati where through connections were available over the Vanderbilt's Big Four Railroad to St. Louis, Indianapolis, and Chicago.

While using its passenger service to publicize itself, C&O's management worked hard to provide for the real wealth of the road by building lines to serve the coal mines that were opening through-

Just five miles from the Virginia border, White Sulphur Springs was always an important passenger stop for C&O mainline trains, taking patrons to and from the world-famous Greenbrier resort hotel, which was owned by C&O after 1910. This 1963 view shows Pullman sleeping cars behind the station and a C&O office car at left on one of the several tracks where sleeping cars could be parked. The mainline with the platform and shed are at right. Regular New York – White Sulphur cars arrived every morning and departed every evening. (Frank Schaeffer photo)

Ronceverte ("Greenbrier" in French) had this large station built about 1917. It was the station for the county seat at Lewisburg (4 miles away) and was headquarters for the 101-mile Greenbrier Branch through that county and Pocahontas county, built in 1900 to haul limber and wood products. In this 1932 scene a local passenger train passes at the gray brick station with its canopy–protected platform. (William Monypeny photo)

No. 1622, another of C&O's mighty H-8 class 2-6-6-6 types roars eastward through Alderson (the only place C&O touches Monroe County) with a fast freight train (note refrigerator cars right behind the locomotive), in December 1946, with a great show of exhaust as it passes along the Greenbrier River. Its freight will terminate at Lynchburg, Richmond, Newport News, Washington, and points east (North) after having originated at Chicago, Columbus, Cincinnati and Kentucky points. (H. H. Harwood Collection)

out the southern West Virginia and eastern Kentucky coal fields. With an easy grade over the Alleghany range, and a water-level down-grade line to the sea at Newport News (opposite Norfolk on Hampton Roads Harbor), which it acquired in 1890, C&O coal could be shipped by water to the northeastern cities at rates that competed with coal produced in Pennsylvania.

C&O's first coal came from mines located on or near its early mainline through the New River gorge west of Hinton and along the Kanawha River. In fact coal had been mined in the Kanawha Valley since the 1790s, and that region of what would become West Virginia was developed because of the salt that could be fairly easily recovered from saline wells along the river. The salt brine had to be boiled so as to produce the "alum salt" that was a key in those days to the preservation of food. Coal was used in the salt furnaces after wood became scarce, but before long it was also transported by boat or barge down the Kanawha and the Ohio to Cincinnati. Therefore, by the time that C&O arrived in the valley the coal industry was already established.

Coal was recognized to exist in good quantities along the New River gorge as well, and the first mines were opened near the station of Quinnimont. Soon after the C&O was opened to traffic a large iron furnace was established at Quinnimont so as to take advantage of the nearby coal reserves for making coke to be used in the iron-making process. The ore was brought in from western Virginia by the C&O and the finished product taken out by rail. Although the iron industry didn't develop, the coking of coal for use in steel making became ever more important in the following decades, and coke was shipped to the great industrial centers.

All this built a foundation for the coal business on the C&O, and by the early 1890s the first branch lines were being built away from the mainline to reach the vast reserves of coal lying under the nearby countryside.

The first ceremonial train across the C&O between Huntinton and Richmond in 1873 arrived at the latter city with a car of West Virginia coal, the first of a flood that was soon released. Through the rest of 1873 C&O handled 22,813 tons of West Virginia coal, and over 34,000 the following year. By 1880 this had reached 333,829 tons and over a million by 1887. This again doubled by 1895 and as the scores of new branches made so many more rich seams available for mining in the following two decades, the quantities multiplied exponentially. Most C&O coal was from West Virginia until just after 1900, when the rich Big Sandy field in eastern Kentucky came into production.

During the era 1895-1920 C&O built scores of coal branches in West Virginia and eastern Kentucky. Since C&O had a line available to the west via the Hocking Valley Railway of Ohio, which it controlled after 1910, it began to ship as much coal west as east. It should be noted here that the Norfolk & Western, which had entered the southern West Virginia coal fields about a decade after C&O, in this same era was doing the same thing as C&O, building coal branches that were providing a flood of coal east to Hampton Roads (Norfolk) and west to Great Lakes shipping (see page 60). Thus, C&O and N&W became and remained actual competitors in the coal markets. The compe-

Lowell, on the Alleghany Subdivision, C&O's mainline between Clifton Forge, Va., and Hinton, W. Va., was a typical rural C&O station building, with decorative verge boards on its gables and board-and-batten siding. It was a combination passenger and freight station with a bay-window office for the agent-operator and three large doors for dispatch and receipt of freight. Although Lowell had a population of only a few score, it served a wide agricultural region. This view is taken from a local passenger train in 1932. (William Monypeny photo)

In this wonderful 1949 photo an eastbound coal train, powered by C&O 2-6-6-6 No. 1643 has just exited Big Bend Tunnel at Talcott. The Great Bend Tunnel, where John Henry of folk-lore fame was supposed to have beaten the steam drill in 1870-71 when C&O was building west, is behind the locomotive. The cut at the top of the hill is state highway 3, and since 1972 a statue of John Henry has stood guard overlooking the tunnels and the verdant valley below. (Charles Kerrigan photo)

tition eastward was further complicated by the arrival of the Virginian Railway in 1909, taking coal from the same region to Norfolk as well (see page 82).

C&O's principal coal districts in West Virginia began just west of Hinton. At Meadow Creek the Nicholas, Fayette & Greenbrier Railroad (NF&G), jointly owned and operated by the C&O and the NYC, joined the main line. On the NF&G the C&O extracted coal from mines closest to its line while NYC operated mines on the western end of the line, connecting with its Gauley Branch out of Gauley Bridge. NYC itself entered the state at Point Pleasant from its Ohio lines, and extended a line up the Kanawha River to Charleston and Gauley Bridge (see page 108). C&O served 24 mines on the NF&G in the Greenbrier field (in Greenbrier, Nicholas, and Fayette counties) according to its 1954 coal mine directory. C&O also served the giant Meadow River Lumber Company sawmill at Rainelle (where the NF&G headquarters, engine terminal and marshalling yard were located). Predecessors of the NF&G were logging roads opened by Meadow River Lumber Company and later purchased by C&O, then consolidated with other lines to form the joint NF&G Railroad in the late 1920s. Meadow River log trains headed for the woods were run over NF&G tracks to get to their various logging branches.

The New River Coal Field was accessed by lines connecting with the C&O main line at Prince, Thurmond, Sewell and Keeney's Creek, and comprised numerous branches that served (in 1954) 41 active mines of various capacities. Attached to the field, but separated by C&O in its accounting was the Winding Gulf Field, which had 14 active mines in 1954, of which several were joint mines served by both C&O and Virginian. Further west

In the era before centralized electronic signal systems C&O and all other railroads had signal towers located where sidings or crossovers from one track to another occurred, and at other points where it was necessary to have an operator who could give trains orders from the dispatcher and could control the switches and signals in the vicinity. In the 1920s C&O started replacing its wooden towers (which it uniquely called "Cabins") with standard brick structures such as this one at Hilldale. (C&O Ry. photo, C&OHS Collection)

along the C&O main line were the Coal River and Kanawha Fields. Branches serving the Kanawha Field connected with the main line at Mt. Carbon, Morris Creek, Pratt, and Cabin Creek Junction. There were (in 1954) 22 active mines in this field.

West of Charleston, along the Kanawha River was the rich Coal River Field, connecting with the main line at St. Albans, and serving 27 active mines. The westernmost C&O coal region in West Virginia was the Logan Field, which connected with the mainline at Barboursville, just a few miles east of Huntington. It had 47 active mines in 1954. C&O, as with N&W, B&O, and WM, also served coal fields in other states. C&O had more mines and produced more coal from its West Virginia branches than from its other operations (princi- pally in eastern Kentucky with a small amount in Ohio).

In the early 1920s C&O came within the con- trol of the Van Sweringen brothers, financial wiz- ards who assembled a huge railroad empire in the 1920s based in Cleveland and originally cen- tered on their first property, the Nickel Plate Road (New York, Cleveland & St. Louis Railroad). C&O soon became the keystone of their empire which included Erie, Pere Marquette, Hocking Valley, C&O, and Nickel Plate as well as part ownership in several other railroads. This is why some of C&O's highest executive offices were moved from Richmond to Cleveland, a city not even on a C&O line. However, this association with the other lines did improve C&O's traffic position, especially in the Midwest.

Looking down on the narrow yard and engine terminal at Hinton in 1947 we see another of the typical H-8 2-6-6-6 types as well as other locomotives. Hinton dispatched coal and other trains east to Clifton Forge, and was the first terminal in West Virginia into which the trains arrived from that point. New River is in the background. West from this point C&O passes through the deep New River Gorge. (B.F. Cutler photo)

West of Hinton at Meadow Creek, C&O's first coal branch diverges from the mainline toward Rainelle. This was operated as a separate company called the Nicholas, Fayette & Greenbrier Railroad, in which the New York Central had a half interest. Both C&O and NYC took coal from mines in the Greenbrier field. C&O's trains took the coal down into the New River Valley using a set of steep loop tracks seen here at Claypool in 1952 with a 2-6-6-2 type bringing empties toward Rainelle. The train will soon be on the track in the foreground. (Bernard Kern photo, C&OHS Collection)

By the 1940s C&O was the largest originator of bituminous coal in the United States (and the world), followed closely by N&W, while B&O and Virginian ran third and fourth.

C&O used its prodigious income from coal to rebuild and upgrade its physical plant over the years, so that by the 1930s it had one of the most solidly built and best maintained railroads in the country, operating with the largest and most modern of locomotives and cars.

It used some of the largest and most powerful locomotives in service anywhere for hauling its heavy coal trains, using the Mallet type (see page 13) extensively, as well as modern "Super Power" locomotives not only for its heaviest coal trains but for its best passenger trains and through freights. C&O had a wide variety of steam locomotive types, many of which were restricted to particular regions of the railway, while neighbor coal hauler N&W tended to concentrate its efforts on developing and building locomotives that had a variety of applications and could be used in dif-

ferent services. West Virginia, of course, was the home of many of the biggest and most powerful of C&O's locomotives. Hauling its eastbound coal C&O had a distinct advantage over any of the other lines because its eastbound crossing of the Alleghany range was the easiest of any. Because of this it could haul heavier loads with less motive power than the other lines, all of which suffered grades three-to-four times steeper.

C&O was late to dieselize, not wanting to change from coal as fuel since it was actively engaged in trying to convince customers that they should stick with coal instead of going to oil or natural gas. As late as 1949 it was receiving new steam locomotives, and in fact its H-6 class 2-6-6-2 types delivered in September 1949 were the very last steam locomotives built commercially for an American railroad. Only N&W had later locomotives, which it built at its own Roanoke Shops through mid-1952.

When C&O finally decided that the economics of the diesel were just too great not to use, it dieselized fairly rapidly. Getting its first diesels in 1949 it was 80% diesel-operated by 1954, and after a brief respite in 1955-56 when some steam was recalled because of increased traffic, all steam was gone by October 1956. A few miles to the south, N&W remained all steam until 1955 and kept some of its most powerful steam operating in the West Virginia coal fields until 1960, the last Class I American railroad to fully dieselize.

C&O's coal business remained strong and in 1958 when it went looking for a merger partner, it began discussions with B&O, which resulted in C&O's control through stock ownership of B&O in 1963. In the following decade the two lines gradually amalgamated their operations and they essentially merged in 1972 into Chessie System Railroads, which Western Maryland joined in 1975. Therefore, by this time the largest railroad operator in West Virginia was C&O/B&O (later Chessie System and now CSX).

C&O had its major locomotive repair shop in

At Sewell, deep into the New River Gorge region, coke ovens are seen here preparing coke for loading into C&O cars at left. Once almost every mine had coke ovens attached, but by the 1940s most coking was being done at the steel mills in large modern plants. The Royalty Smokeless Coal Company's operation here, photographed in 1954, was the last along the C&O mainline. Coal originated on the narrow-gauge short line Mann's Creek railroad and was dumped through the tipples seen in the background. (C&O Ry. photo, COHS Collection)

The Mann's Creek railroad was a narrow gauge line that delivered coal to the C&O mainline at Sewell. It served mines owned by the Babcock Coal & Coke Co., located just up the Mann's Creek canyon from that point, and became rather famous because it persisted in steam operation well into the 1950s, using Shay geared locomotives. This photo shows one of its small Shays, with all its lettering worn away and its running board filled with grease cans and tools, at Cliff Top in 1953. (T. L. Wise photo)

West Virginia at Huntington, which was at about the center of its system. The huge facility was gradually upgraded and expanded so that it became one of the largest steam locomotive repair facilities in the eastern U. S. This shop was later converted to diesel repair and remains today as one of three shop facilities on the huge CSX system. It also headquartered its coal department and its finance department at Huntington in the 1920-1960s era, as well as its engineering headquarters from 1960 until the mid-1980s. It was the only one of West Virginia's major railroads to have a large part of its operational headquarters and maintenance shops within the state's borders.

The city of Huntington itself owes its existence to the coming of the C&O in the early 1870s when C&O president C. P. Huntington bought the land on which the city is situated, and sold it off to help finance his railroad venture. Because of its good location on railroads and waterways, Huntington became an industrial center of considerable importance and one of West Virginia's largest cities. C&O's presence was always the key to the city's development.

C&O also had major terminals at Hinton and Handley, and many smaller yards and engine servicing facilities in the coal fields areas such as Peach Creek (Logan), Danville, Cane Fork, St. Albans, Quinnimont, Raleigh, and Rainelle.

C&O had a great folk tradition centered in West Virginia. No less than a dozen folksongs exist, dealing with C&O subjects (wrecks and accidents) in West Virginia. "Wreck on the C&O" about George Alley and the wreck of the *Fast Flying Virginian* near Hinton in 1890 was once one of the best known railroad folksongs in America.

However, the most important folk hero of the C&O was John Henry. Hundreds of versions of the folk ballad "John Henry" have been collected and catalogued, four full length books have been written about him, and he has been the subject of hundreds of articles and mentions in books, yet we are not sure if he existed, who exactly he was, or if he really had his battle with the new steam drill. According to most of the song versions, John Henry was a black ex-slave who came to Great Bend Tunnel at Talcott, West Virginia, with C&O crews in 1870 to drill through the spur of the mountain that forced the Greenbrier River into a "great bend." The 6500-foot tunnel was drilled under the most primitive and arduous conditions, and according to most versions, the early steam-powered drill was used on the job, but John Henry taking pride in his ability claimed he could drill better and faster than the new machine.

A contest was supposed to have been set up in which John Henry, according to the song "made his fifteen feet, while the steam drill made only nine." This would have been very possible since the steam drill (predecessor to today's pneumatic drills) was prone to broken drill bits, causing delays. After the contest, John Henry was supposed to have died of exhaustion. From that time forward wherever there were African-American laborers working on railroads or in the fields, they loved to sing the ballad of John Henry and his great feat. In the last few years, the U. S. Postal Service issued a stamp commemorating John Henry. Only in the last few years a new book has been published which postulates that John Henry's real work was at Lewis Tunnel, East Alleghany, Virginia, about a mile east of the West Virginia border on the C&O mainline. Regardless of this, John Henry is and probably will always be the great folk hero of West Virginia: a symbol of man against machine, the archetype of the human against the inhumanity of encroaching technology, and the emblem of manhood in the machine age.

As noted before, White Sulphur Springs was a center for much of C&O's most lucrative passenger business. When M. E. Ingalls became president of the C&O in 1889, he wanted to buy the hotel because it appealed to him, but it was not available, therefore he moved on to Virginia's Hot Springs, where he built the fabulous Homestead Hotel. Later, in 1910, C&O management was able to acquire the White Sulphur Springs property and built the new Greenbrier Hotel. With its heritage, it became one of the great resorts of the eastern U. S. The bulk of its clientele came from the great Eastern cities, and they came via C&O's trains. Regular Pullman sleeping car lines were established which delivered and picked up cars at White Sulphur Springs on a regular basis, and throughout the years, but most especial-

This mine tipple at Nuttall is typical of those along the wild and impressive scenery of the New River. The C&O mainline passes under it in this 1947 photo. (C&O Ry. photo, C&OHS Collection)

ly in the era 1920-1969, large numbers of special movements of cars came to and from the hotel from both east and west, sometimes added to regular trains, and sometimes as a special or even groups of special trains. There was no other location in West Virginia that had the passenger attraction that the Greenbrier did, and C&O used it not only to gen-

The huge depot at Thurmond was the focus of much activity in the great days of the New River coal field's exploitation. In the 1920s the station billed more freight than any other location on the C&O (all the coal from mines on the nearby branch lines). This wonderful night photo shows the station before it was completely restored to its 1920s appearance as part of the National River. It is today a center of tourist visitation in the park. (Ron Piskor photo)

These two photos show Thurmond's engine terminal in May 1953. The first, looking west shows the two stall engine house with H-4 2-6-6-2 No. 1490 waiting to enter. The other is looking east with a couple of engines beside the town on the left and the water tanks in the distance. The station is hidden behind the two locomotives. (D. Wallace Johnson photos)

erate that extra business, but as part of its publicity about itself. The Green-brier was C&O's "crown jewel." CSX retained the hotel until 2009.

This interesting view from inside a tipple looking at the loading process as a C&O 2-6-6-2 mine shifter prepares to pick up loads at the Crab Orchard tipple of the Gulf Mining Company in October 1945. Note the rough run-of-the-mine coal in the car at the far left. Each chute generally had a different grade, or size of coal. (C&O Ry. photo, C&OHS Collection)

Although many of the mines served by C&O were drift mines, which entered a hillside at the point of a coal vein, some were shaft mines such as this one at Lochgelly, near Beckley. Note the tower with pulley which took miners and coal up and down the shaft. There are three different grades of coal in the hopper cars. The mine employee is using a hand brake to allow loaded cars to drift away from the tipple where they will await pickup by a C&O mine shifter. (C&O Ry. photo, C&OHS Collection)

At the coal marshalling yard of Raleigh, C&O Mallet types 2-6-6-2 locomotives get service before heading out as mine-run shifters in the early 1950s. C&O loved the flexible, powerful Mallets for the coal branch mine shifters. (C&O Ry. photo, C&OHS Collection)

C&O's Piney Creek branch extended from the mainline at Prince to the coal marshalling yard at Raleigh, near Beckley, where many other coal-originating branches radiated. Here two class H-4 2-6-6-2 compound articulateds (Mallets) are handling a loaded coal train coming down the branch to Prince and then one mile on to the yard at Quinnimont, where the coal will wait to be picked up by a mainline coal train to Hinton. (C&O Ry. photo, C&OHS Collection)

Way down below we see some C&O GP9 diesels with a train of loaded hoppers headed for Gulf Switch in the rugged Winding Gulf district. The train is passing under the track of the Virginian Railway which enters the tunnel in the center. Eventually the train will be on the track in the foreground. (Gene Huddleston photo)

51

The Winding Gulf Coals, Inc. tipple at Tams, W. Va. Is seen here in June 1954. Typical of a tipple on the C&O in this region, it is of wooden frame construction with board-and-batten siding. Other tipples often had corrugated siding over either wood or steel framing. (C&O Ry. photo, C&OHS Collection)

This tipple of the C. H. Mead Company at Mead, W. Va. on C&O's Stone Coal Branch in Raleigh County, was a joint mine served by both C&O and Virginian (note cars from both roads). Its tipple is of the corrugated siding construction with tracks for loading four grades of coal concurrently. The mine head itself is on the hillside to the right with a conveyor taking the coal to the tipple for cleaning and sorting. (C&O Ry. photo, C&OHS Collection)

This famous scene is from the Hawks Nest State Park overlook, as C&O's west-bound passenger Train, No. 3, The Fast Flying Virginian crosses the river below making its daily trip between Washington and Cincinnati. This whole region today is encompassed by the New River Gorge National River park. (Elmer Treloar photo)

Train No. 6, the eastbound FFV rounds a curve in the New River Gorge in September 1959. The train, operating between Cincinnati and Washington is handled by three E8 diesels and has a Railway Post Office "apartment" car, a three-door express car, and a two-door working baggage car in front of its passenger carrying cars. The RPO apartment meant that only a portion of the car was devoted to en-route sorting of U. S. Mail and the balance of the car was available for express or storage mail. The rocky New River was always one of the scenic attractions of C&O passenger service. (C&O Ry. photo, C&OHS Collection)

There are a couple of different grades of coal in the loaded cars at the Mt. Carbon Fuel Company's #3 mine at Decota, W. Va. In 1954, on the Republic Subdivision of the Cabin Creek Branch. (C&O Ry. photo, C&OHS Collection).

53

Opposite Top: Typical of C&O's many branch line trains is the Coal River local arriving at St. Albans after an all-day trip up the various branches of that district and back. The ancient 4-4-2 Atlantic type has just two cars in tow, a M&E (Mail and Express) car with half its space devoted to a Railway Post Office operation and the other for baggage, storage mail, and express, while a straight coach follows. Branch line trains were money losers and C&O eliminated most of them in the decade following WWII. (C.A. Brown photo, C&OHS Collection)

Opposite Bottom: The mainline of the Kanawha Subdivision, running from Handley, W. Va. all the way to Ashland, Kentucky, was a favored haunt of the K-4 Class 2-8-4 "Kanawha" type locomotive, of which C&O bought 90 between 1943 and 1948. Here No. 2746 storms east with a coal train in the fall of 1953 near Barboursville. (C&O Ry. photo, C&OHS Collection)

C&O erected this impressive brick station in 1906 to serve Charleston, West Virginia's capital city. It had waiting rooms on both floors and was a major passenger traffic point on the C&O in West Virginia. (TLC Collection).

The Charleston station in later days from the track side looking west. The baggage truck loaded with mail was a common sight even at this later date as C&O trains carried a huge volume of mail to and from Charleston. (T. W. Dixon, Jr. Collection)

Just 10 miles west of Charleston is St. Albans which is the junction point for the rich Coal River District of the C&O, still an important coal traffic region today for CSX. This early 1950s photo shows a K-4 class 2-8-4 "Kanawha Type" headed east probably with a coal train, while another heads west (to the right), and the small single-stall engine house hosts a 2-8-0 for use in switching and local trains on the branch. The large 500-ton concrete coaling station was typical of those on the C&O. (Gary Huddleston photo)

Hostler (one who moves locomotives around the engine terminal as they are serviced) and engineer talk at the Peach Creek engine terminal at Logan in 1943. The pair look the part of railroad men that has come down to us today in lore and nostalgic memory. (C&O Ry. photo, C&OHS Collection)

C&O's hugely productive Logan Coal Field was reached by its Logan branch running south from Barboursville into Logan, Mingo, and Wyoming Counties. The hub of activity on the many branches in this region was at Peach Creek yard , adjacent to the city of Logan. Here the C&O official photographer has captured the coaling station and several locomotives ready for action in 1946. The big flat-face locomotive in the distance is a powerful 0-10-0 switcher used to move heavy cuts of coal cars. (C&O Ry. photo, C&OHS Collection)

The Elk Creek Coal Company's large modern tipple and preparation plant was at Emmett, W. Va., on the Elk Creek branch off the Logan Subdivision and is seen here in 1954. (C&O Ry. photo, C&OHS Collection)

Double heading 2-6-6-2 Mallets pull a string of 17 loads on the Trace Fork branch in May 1953. Coal coming from the Logan field was sent both east to dumping at Newport News and west for dumping at Toledo. The Logan field is still very active for CSX traffic. (C&OHS Collection)

At Huntington C&O installed a locomotive repair facility in the early 1870s. In time, it became the railway's principal shop for heavy repair. This aerial view from 1945 shows the complex at its height, when it had a huge employment and was the bulwark of Huntington's economy. The same facility is used by CSX today as one of its major locomotive repair shops. (C&O Ry. photo, C&OHS Collection)

Taking wheels off and putting them on a big steam locomotive was always one of the most impressive parts of a steam shop work. Here a C&O 2-8-2 Mikado type is held in the air by a large overhead crane as machinists roll a set of driving wheels away to be reworked and reapplied, in the war year of 1943. (C&O Ry. photo, C&OHS Collection)

In another 1943 photo we see a powerful steam hammer in operation in the blacksmith shop at Huntington. Steam Locomotives required constant renewal and repair and most parts were made by the shops. (C&O Ry. photo, C&OHS Collection)

In 1954 the Huntington shop was converted from steam to diesel repair, as this 1956 photo attests. The erecting floor, once populated by steam locomotives, is seen with a variety of the early diesels under repair. (C&O Ry. photo, C&OHS Collection)

Huntington's large passenger station and office building was erected in 1913 and served the many passenger trains operating on the mainline and on the Logan branch. Locomotives were often changed here and consists adjusted. This building is still standing, with the platform canopy removed, now in use as a CSX office building. (C&O Ry., C&OHS Collection)

The last station stop for C&O trains before crossing the Big Sandy River into Kentucky was at Kenova (named after Kentucky-Ohio-West Virginia), since it was near the junction of the three states. Here C&O local Train No. 7 pauses in September 1947. The platform above served the Norfolk & Western mainline, which crossed here, and the lower platform also served the B&O Ohio River Division until 195_, so Kenova was a "Union Station" serving all three roads. (TLC Collection)

This 1948 photo shows a C&O passenger train, powered by one of the road's huge 4-6-4 Hudson type locomotives, crossing the Big Sandy Bridge leaving West Virginia and about to enter Kentucky for the balance of its trip down the south bank of the Ohio River and across that stream into Cincinnati. (C&O Ry. photo, C&OHS Collection)

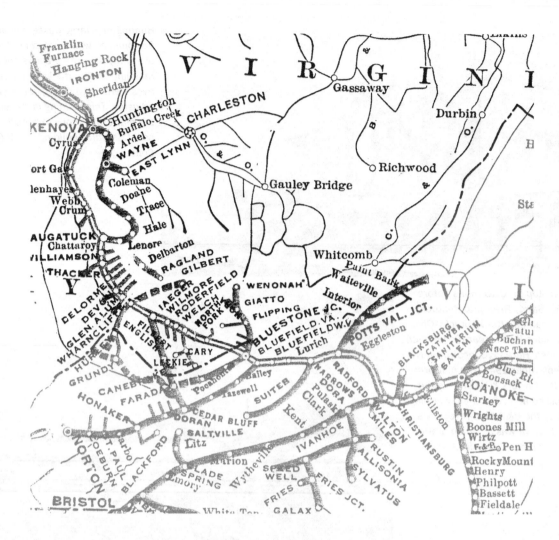

Traveling west on the Norfolk & Western main line, the Virginia/West Virginia border is crossed near milepost 331 (measured from Norfolk) between the N&W stations of Glen Lyn, Va., and Willis, W. Va. From that point the line hugs the southern West Virginia border for about 20 miles to the terminal/yard at Bluefield. This photo shows N&W Class-A 2-6-6-4 simple articulated No. 1202 at speed with an eastbound coal train in June 1958 in the last years of steam operations, is on its way east from Bluefield en route to Roanoke. Its coal will ultimately reach Lambert's Point piers in Norfolk to be dumped into oceangoing and coastwise shipping. (J. Parker Lamb Photo)

Norfolk and Western

One of the five Class I railroads which had operations in West Virginia and which had an important effect on the state's development, the N&W began initially in eastern Virginia and didn't reach into West Virginia until 1881.

When one thinks of the Norfolk & Western and its history today, the word "coal" is paramount. It was the hauling of this "burning rock" that made the N&W the powerhouse of 20th Century railroading that led to today's giant Norfolk Southern Railroad. Significantly, it was mainly West Virginia coal that was the traffic which allowed N&W to become the giant that it was.

The original lineal predecessor of N&W was the Norfolk & Petersburg Railroad, which was chartered in 1850. In 1853 construction began on the line between the seaport city and Petersburg, situated just south of Richmond. While it was being built, the Southside Railroad built a line west from Petersburg to the fledging industrial and agricultural city of Lynchburg. The N&P connected with the Southside at Petersburg August 10, 1858, and through trains were thereafter operated.

The Virginia & Tennessee Railroad began at Lynchburg and built to Bristol, Virginia/Tennessee. The three roads gave great service to the Confederacy during the War Between the States. After the war, administration and operation of all three railroads was consolidated when William Mahone was elected president of all three concurrently. Then in 1870, the companies were merged into the Atlantic, Mississippi & Ohio Railroad Company, the name also reflecting a much broader ambition. The new company had mainlines of 408 miles, all in Virginia.

As with many railroads, the AM&O suffered from financial problems following the financial panic of 1873 and was in receivership after 1876. In 1881, the line was sold to Philadelphia financier C. H. Clark, who reorganized the company as the Norfolk & Western Railroad. Clark also gained control of the Shenandoah Valley Railroad, then building a line up the Shenandoah Valley of Virginia, connecting with the N&W at what is now Roanoke, Virginia. Clark was aware of rich bituminous coal deposits in western Virginia and West Virginia and aimed at using the two lines to

Bluefield served not only as a terminal point for N&W in West Virginia, but dispatched trains to and from southwestern Virginia as well. Here a Pacific (4-6-2) type locomotive is taking a passenger train out of Bluefield headed for Norton, Virginia, on the N&W's Clinch Valley district in June 1958. (H. H. Harwood, Jr. photo)

exploit these resources.

N&W built a new line westward to reach the best of these coal fields, arriving at what is now Bluefield, West Virginia (in 1881), and the nearby town of Pocahontas, in 1883. In the first year of this new operation N&W hauled over 81,000 tons of coal and another 23,000 tons of coke from this area, and the pattern of the future was set.

At the same time, the Chesapeake & Ohio (C&O), running across southern West Virginia north of the N&W route, extended its line in the east to Newport News on the great deepwater port of Hampton Roads, opposite Norfolk. At Newport News it erected a pier for dumping coal into barges and ships to be transported mainly to northeastern cities. N&W, sensing the need to compete, built its first coal pier at Lambert's Point in Norfolk. The two railways competed in shipping coal from these two terminals for the balance of their lives and into the era of their successors down to the present day. After the Virginian Railway built its piers on the Norfolk side it became the third competitor in this trade (see page 82).

In 1886 N&W's five-foot track gauge was changed to the standard of 4-feet, 8-½-inches, along with all the other southern railroads that had been built to the broad gauge. Then, in 1887 the Clinch Valley extension was built into the coal fields of southwestern Virginia, extending about 100 miles west of Bluefield, to Norton, Va. In 1890 N&W gained control of the Scioto Valley Railroad from Portsmouth to Columbus, in Ohio, hoping to eventually use it as a westward extension, but it did not physically connect with N&W at all.

In 1891-92 the 191-mile gap through West Virginia was completed, including a bridge across the Ohio River at Kenova, W. Va. This gave N&W a western outlet for its coal and a competitive advantage over C&O, which had western connections at Cincinnati, but no good route to Great Lakes shipping in Ohio. During the 1890s and well into the 20th Century many branches were built in southwestern Virginia and West Virginia to reach the rich coal veins that lay beneath the mountains of these regions, and the coal business expanded exponentially.

Through the 1890s N&W also merged the Shenandoah Valley line into its company, purchased the Lynchburg and Durham and the Roanoke Southern (with its line to Winston-Salem, N. C.). Unfortunately, this expansion came at the time that another financial panic and depression seized the United States in 1893. In 1896 the N&W Rail*road* was sold at foreclosure and was reorganized as the N&W Rail*way*. From that point onward the company, supported by its huge coal traffic, became a financial giant.

Above: Bluefield and Williamson were N&W's two principal coal field marshalling yards and division points. Bluefield straddled the Virginia/West Virginia border and at this point the N&W yard is actually in both states as is part of the city (actually two cities, one in each state). However, the West Virginia side was the important residential and business district and it was here that the late 19th century N&W depot was placed. In this 1941 scene, the fine old stone building was well kept and visited by at least six mainline and several branch line trains per day. (TLC Collection)

Below: Interior of the Bluefield passenger station waiting room after it was remodeled and modernized in the summer of 1941. Only the old style bench breaks with the otherwise "Art Moderne" atmosphere. (TLC Collection)

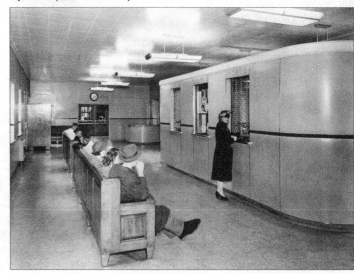

Mainline passenger service through Bluefield consisted of N&W's name trains operating between Norfolk and Cincinnati. Here the Pocahontas (Train No. 4) is rolling eastward just out of Bluefield in June 1958. This was in the last days when N&W used its fabulous J-class 4-8-4 streamlined locomotives on its name trains. No. 600, the first of the class (built in Roanoke shops 1941) has charge of this train. Three express cars are visible in front of the RPO, just rounding the curve. (H. H. Harwood, Jr. Photo)

In 1897 N&W's Roanoke Shops were created out of the former Roanoke Machine Works, and these shops became one of America's most famous locomotive construction and repair facilities, rivaling Pennsylvania's famous Altoona Works. N&W began to build its own locomotives and after 1927 it built all its new engines, buying none from the commercial builders.

In 1900 the Pennsylvania Railroad bought control of both N&W and C&O in order to eliminate the competition that West Virginia coal from these two lines, shipped to the northeast via Hampton Roads, was creating for the Pennsylvania's own on-line coal. C&O and N&W coal was actually cheaper in the big cities than the PRR's coal, hauled a much shorter distance. However, this opened up the Great Lakes traffic for N&W through its coal being routed over the PRR north of Columbus.

PRR retained control of C&O for only a few years, but held its N&W interests until 1964. Though PRR didn't exercise much direct control over N&W operations in later years, its influence manifested itself in the signaling systems that were similar to PRR's and the Tuscan Red color of N&W's passenger cars, which was a standard of the PRR.

In 1901 N&W acquired its line from Portsmouth to Cincinnati (built originally in the 1880s as the narrow gauge Cincinnati, Portsmouth & Virginia Railroad), as well as numerous other short lines. But one of the major changes of the era was the complete realignment of its route from Naugatuck to Kenova, in southern West Virginia. The main line was relocated and built with better grades and curvature, hugging the Tug Fork and Big Sandy rivers which formed the border between Kentucky and West Virginia.

This overhead view shows several big N&W articulated locomotives at the engine terminal ready-track servicing area at Bluefield in July 1956. The city's main business district is to the right, abutting the yard. Looming in the distant background through the haze is the giant coaling station, the last large locomotive coaling station built. (Joe Schmitz Photo)

One of N&W's giants, Y6 class 2-8-8-2 compound articulated (Mallet) No. 2106, is ready to take an empty hopper train out of Bluefield on January 23, 1959, as it had been doing since it was built at Roanoke in late 1931, but it wouldn't be around much longer. Just six months later it was scrapped. Ominously, behind it is the new diesel fuel pad servicing facility that replaced the large and elaborate steam facilities. (Jay Williams Collection)

Many other improvements were made, branches built, and a portion of the line's most torturous grade in West Virginia was electrified.

Between 1915 and 1924 N&W electrified its main line between Bluefield and Iaeger, W. Va., about 56 miles. This allowed electric locomotives, drawing their power from overhead lines, to supplement steam on the heaviest coal trains over Elkhorn grade, N&W's steepest and most difficult area for taking coal eastward from the West Virginia fields. Because of N&W's success with its electric operation by increasing tonnage and speed, the Virginian Railway decided to electrify a much longer part of its mainline from the coal fields (see page 85).

By about 1925, the modern N&W as it was known throughout most of the 20th Century was in place and its coal business continued to expand over time, both eastbound and westbound.

N&W's coal fields lines in West Virginia were divided by districts, as they were on the other major coal haulers. Between Bluefield and Welch was the Pocahontas District, the most famous of N&W's coal fields. According to N&W's 1951 Coal Mine Directory, 48 mines were in this field, all except five of which were in West Virginia. West of this was the Tug River District between Welch and Iaeger on the main line, with 18 active mines listed in 1951.

Between Iaeger and Williamson on the main line, the Thacker District straddled the West Virginia, Virginia, and Kentucky borders, and showed 50 active mines in 1951, about half (28) of which were in Virginia or Kentucky. However, some of the coal produced in the Kentucky and Virginia mines was still funneled through West Virginia, especially if it was westbound.

The western most of the N&W

coal districts in West Virginia was the Kenova District between Williamson and Kenova. This field had only 12 active mines, 11 in West Virginia and one in Kentucky, according to the 1951 directory. N&W's other coal field districts were in southwestern Virginia.

With its huge cash reserves from coal business, N&W rebuilt its roadway, tunnels, terminals, shops, yards, and other facilities so that by the 1920s they were among the best in the country. It bought its last steam locomotive from a commercial builder in 1927 and thereafter relied on Roanoke Shops to build all its new steam locomotives. N&W became legendary as the consummate practitioner of the locomotive builder's art, and these talented managers and workers turned out some of the best steam locomotives of all time in the following decades. To complement this, N&W practised probably the best use of steam, tailoring its locomotives to its particular needs, so that by the post-WWII era, when all other railroads were rushing headlong into dieselization as fast as they could, N&W continued building steam. It was the last Class I railroad in America to dieselize, and didn't drop the fires of its last steamers until early May 1960. This was possible because N&W used its ultra-modern and very versatile steam much as other roads used their diesels, dispatching and ser-

Bluefield's ultra-modern "lubratorium" steam servicing building is in the background of Y3-class 2-8-8-2 No. 2040 on September 1, 1957. N&W perfected the compound articulated with its successive Y-classes starting in 1910 but really getting a boost with this 1919 design, which was still going strong almost 30 years later, but it's end would come three months after this photo was taken. (TLC Collection).

vicing them on a turn-around time that was equal to diesels. But eventually, as good as N&W steam was, it had to fall to diesels for many reasons.

In 1950 the steep eastbound Elkhorn line was relocated across the adjacent valley, a new Elkhorn tunnel bored, and the electrified territory

In this 1956 view of the Bluefield terminal, the large old Railroad YMCA building is the dominant feature overlooking the ready tracks jammed with N&W's steam giants. The YMCA had a railroad department which provided a good wholesome place to stay, eat, and relax for crews away from their home terminals. Most railroads provided the buildings and utilities. After all, they would have to have supplied a bunk house facility if the Y wasn't available. (Joe Schmitz Photo)

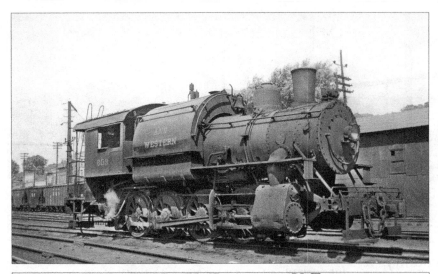

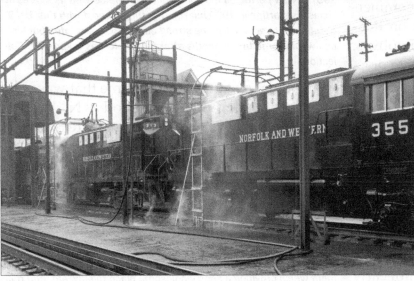

was eliminated. This was one of the few instances in which a steam railroad line was electrified and then later returned to steam operation.

In the 1914-1920 period, the flow of coal westward greatly increased so that it eventually became much larger than the original eastward traffic. Eastbound traffic increased after World War II, when demand for export coal grew. Gaining the better eastward gradient of the Virginian mainline became even more important to N&W than it had been when it first tried to lease the Virginian in 1925, and finally in 1959 N&W was allowed to buy the Virginian.

In the era up to the 1960s, N&W concentrated much of its attention on its operations in the coal fields of southwestern Virginia and West Virginia, and it was only as it began to buy other railroads in the Midwest that it began to become a more diversified operation.

By 1964 N&W encompassed its original line, the Virginian, plus the Nickel Plate Railroad, Wabash Railroad, Akron, Canton & Youngstown Railroad, Atlantic & Danville Railroad, and others, which had been acquired in the 1960s. In 1982 N&W merged with the Southern Railway to form Norfolk Southern, the company which now operates the N&W's and Virginian's former lines in West Virginia, as well as the NYC's old Kanawha & Michigan lines, which were acquired in 1999 when NS and CSX took over former Conrail lines.

In West Virginia, N&W had two primary terminals and yards, one at Bluefield, which actually straddled the West Virginia/Virginia border, and at Williamson. Between these two points lay most coal branches and mining operations of the N&W. The railroad had other coal fields which it entered in southwestern Virginia and also into eastern Kentucky, but by far the greatest amount of its coal came from the area between Bluefield and Williamson and up to Kenova, in southwestern West Virginia, mainly in Mercer, McDowell, Wyoming and Mingo counties.

N&W's electrification extended about 56 miles from Bluefield to Iaeger, W. Va., and was partially placed in operation in 1915. It encompassed the heavy eastbound Elkhorn grade and was an integral part of operations until the new Elkhorn realignment allowed its elimination in 1950. Class LC2 jack-shaft box cab electric 2514 is seen here at Bluefield yard July 27, 1949. Built in 1925 it was about to end its service. (August A. Thieme Photo)

Class LC1 Electric No. 2506 is pulling a heavy coal train toward Bluefield in this 1940s photo. Four of the box cab units are in service in this scene. (TLC Collection)

A set of two N&W LC2 electric units (2512) power an eastbound coal train near Bluestone Junction, nearing the end of electric territory at Bluefield in December 1929 (N&W Ry. TLC Collection)

LC1 class N&W jack-shaft electric set No. 2504 is seen at the end of its career under the soon-to-be-removed wires at Bluefield yard July 27, 1949. Part of the first (1915) group of N&W electrics, it served another year until the end of electrified operation. (August A. Thieme Photo)

This late 1930s photo shows The Pocahontas, then the flagship of the N&W passenger fleet, with its eight-car heavyweight train operating over the electrified territory just west of Maybeury, W. Va. Electric locomotives were not used for passenger trains except in unusual circumstances. (N&W Ry. Photo, Jay Williams Collection)

No. 2196 was one of N&W's last new steam locomotives, a class Y6b 2-8-8-2, incorporating more than 30 years of experience in developing the 2-8-8-2 compound articulated. The 2196 was turned out of Roanoke shops in 1951 and would be one of the last retired, in 1960. Here it is making a grand show with a fast freight train just west of Bluefield in August 1954. (D. Wallace Johnson Photo)

Just west of Bluefield, the Bluestone Branch tapped into coal seams primarily in Mercer County and had eight spurs running to mines along the way. In 1950, when N&W still supplied local passenger service on its coal branches, a single set of equipment consisting of a Pacific type locomotive, a mail and express car and a coach operated as seven different numbered trains as it served the branches, leaving Bluestone Junction at 9:45 a.m. and getting back at 3:15 p.m. The equipment then went to Bluefield for the night. Here No. 60 is at Giatto more than half way through its day's activities. (TLC Collection).

Exhaust is seen from the Worthington feedwater heater in front of the rear cylinder as N&W Y6 No. 2133 climbs the grade into Bluefield at the summit of Great Flattop Mountain. The Mallet has an auxiliary tender which N&W added to many of its locomotives after 1952 so as to eliminate some water stops. (Railroad Avenue Enterprises Collection)

Nearing the new Elkhorn Tunnel, west of Bluefield, on February 1, 1958, Y6-class 2-8-8-2 No. 2143 displays a heavy exhaust. After the mainline was realigned to a better grade and a new tunnel bored, N&W eliminated its electrified territory in 1950. (TLC Collection)

J-class 4-8-4 No. 612 has an westbound passenger train exiting the new Elkhorn Tunnel in August 1956. On this day the train is carrying some deadhead coaches up front. (H. Reid Photo)

The Powhatan Arrow, Train No. 26 eastbound has J-class No. 611 for power as it crosses the Tug Fork near Welch in the summer of 1957. The Arrow carried a Railway Post Office car only west of Bluefield. (Gene Huddleston Photo)

Well down the Elkhorn grade on its western approach was the coal marshalling yard and mine shifter terminal at Iaeger. Much smaller than Bluefield or Williamson, it was the third important coal terminal on N&W in West Virginia. Mine shifters based here served numerous tipples on many branches nearby. This night photo shows Y6 No. 2154 under the small coaling station with the long frame engine house in the background. (TLC Collection)

Inside the Iaeger engine house, Y6 No. 2154 is being serviced with two other locomotives sit at the right. (TLC Collection)

Another view shows Y6 No. 2153 outside the Iaeger engine house, ready for a mine shifter run in the mist of early morning. This shows the board-and-batten engine house with its monitor roof, in a scene very typical of coal fields railroading on N&W in the 1940s-1950s. (TLC Collection)

A Y-class 2-8-8-2 backs its load of coal on the Dry Fork Branch headed to Auville yard at Iaeger. As with all mine run shifters, the locomotive left the yard in the morning with empty cars which it left at various mines while picking up their loads. (Gary E. Huddleston Photo)

This impressive tipple of the Bottom Creek Coal & Coke Company at Vivian had tracks to load five grades of coal at a time. Note that the grades of coal go from the huge lumps of run-of-the-mine at right to tiny pea size at left. (TLC Collection)

Inside tipples the coal was cleaned and then separated by size and the impurities were removed. Much of the work was done automatically by use of sieves, but picking tables with men working by hand were also an integral part of the operation. (TLC Collection)

The screening of coal can be seen well in this tipple interior photo. Note that the incoming coal from the mine is passing over grates with various sized holes, allowing the coal of different sizes to fall through. The men at the picking table seem to be handling large blocks. (TLC Collection)

The Yukon Mine at Yukon, W. Va. is seen in this view and the method of filling cars is quite evident. The empties (background left) are positioned on one side of a tipple. They are then run under the tipple by means of using a hand brake (the yard being on a slight grade), or they were pulled by a pulley system. (TLC Collection)

Once the coal was separated and cleaned in the tipple it was sent down to the waiting cars by means of conveyors. This scene is at the Pond Creek Pocahontas Company at Hartley, W. Va. (TLC Collection)

Egg size coal is being loaded at Crystal Block Mining Company Gates Mine at Lobata, W. Va. This type of coal was popular for stoves and home heating as well as industries with stoker-fired boilers. (TLC Collection)

United Pocahontas Coal Company had this large tipple at Crumpler, W. Va. The raw coal is seen coming from the mine head in small mine cars, which then enter the tipple and are dumped into the sorting, washing, and separating area. (TLC Collection)

The Crystal Block Coal Company's mine and tipple at Matewan, W. Va., showing strings of loaded N&W hopper cars with different sizes of coal ready to be picked up by the next mine run shifter. The coal is coming to the tipple from the drift mine mouth far up the hill at left. (TLC Collection)

The large yard, engine terminal, and roundhouse at Williamson was a key part of N&W's coal fields system. This 1946 overhead view, taken after extensive modernization, shows the large roundhouse at left, and to its right is the long brick "lubratorium" building where locomotives were given full lubrication in record time. Beyond it the ash pit area, ready track and to the far right the large coaling station. (N&W Ry., TLC Collection)

Another view 1946 of the Williamson terminal after its renovation and installation of high capacity, streamlined servicing facilities, showing the ready tracks, and cinder pits, with the lubratorium building in the background. This small area allowed N&W to service steam locomotives between runs on an average of about an hour, which was comparable with contemporary diesel servicing times. N&W held on to steam so much longer than other roads partly because of its highly efficient servicing. (N&W Ry., TLC Collection)

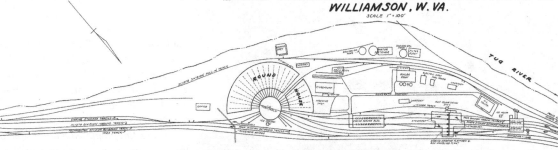

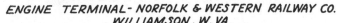

ENGINE TERMINAL- NORFOLK & WESTERN RAILWAY CO.
WILLIAMSON, W. VA.
SCALE 1"=100'

Map showing the "new" (1946) Williamson terminal layout after many of the old facilities had been removed and the streamlined lubratorium and ready tracks installed. (N&W Ry., TLC Collection)

Inside the Williamson lubratorium building, hoses were positioned so lubrication could be done on any type locomotive without moving it, which greatly improved turn-around times. Here workers lubricate an A-class 2-6-6-4 simple articulated, one of N&W's modern "Super Power" steamers. Facilities such as this were installed in the late 1940s at all major N&W terminals. (N&W Ry., TLC Collection)

An impressive night scene at the Williamson ready track and lubratorium with big articulateds at the ready. (N&W Ry., TLC Collection)

J-class 4-8-4 No. 605 pauses with N&W's workhorse eastbound Cavalier at Williamson in April 1957. The Pocahontas carried N&W's major sleeping car trade and the Powhatan Arrow was the fast daylight coach streamliner, but the Cavalier at this time handled a great deal of local business, including much mail and express. (TLC Collection)

No. 603 has the Powhatan Arrow in tow between Williamson and Ft. Gay, W. Va., in this 1958 photo after the once all-coach and no-head end traffic train had gotten its RPO, storage mail, and combination cars. (Jay Williams Collection)

Y-6 No. 2139 is shifting cars at the Island Creek Coal Co. mine at Ragland at the end of the Lenore Branch in December 1958, the cold air condensing the steam exhaust into a white plume. (Gary Huddleston photo)

Y6a 2-8-8-2 No. 2166 is stopped at Kermit while doing duties on a mine shifter as its crew takes lunch at a local restaurant in December 1956. (Gary Huddleston Photo)

Leased Atlantic Coast Line E7 and RF&P E8 bring the eastbound Cavalier into Kenova in October 1958 with a long string of mail and express cars ahead of its coaches. The big bridge in the background is across the Ohio River, so Kenova is the westernmost station on the N&W in West Virginia. (H. H. Harwood, Jr. Photo)

N&W caboose #518402 brings up the rear of a coal drag coming off the Dry Fork Branch, with the crew looking forward to ending their run. The Iaeger roundhouse can be seen at the left, and catenary for operation of the electric locomotives is still up, dating the photo to about 1941. (N&W Photo)

In the foreground is Z1a 2-6-6-2 #1362 and in the background is a Y4 2-8-8-2. Both appear to have trains under way at Bluefield, probably sometime in the late 1930s or early 1940s. (TLC Collection)

Norfolk & Western Extra 2123 East puts on quite a show as it departs Matewan, W.Va., with eight cars and caboose on Feb. 11, 1960. The Williamson-to-Iaeger, W.Va., crew had stopped to set off a few cars and inspect the locomotive — giving the photographer a chance to meet them. Fireman Sam Noe told him to have his camera ready for a great show of smoke and cinders from Class Y6 2-8-8-2 locomotive No. 2123, and he was not disappointed. Less than three months later, N&W's regular steam operations were history. (Larry K. Fellure Sr. photo, Bob Withers Collection)

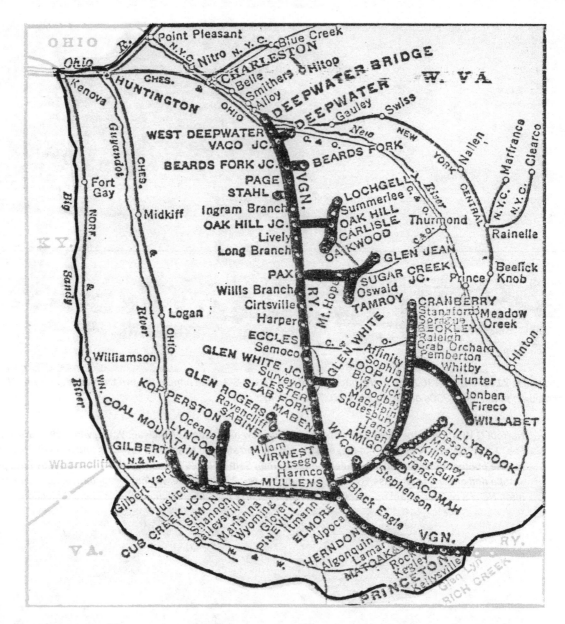

Virginian

The Virginian Railway has its origins in West Virginia and it may be said that its sole purpose was to haul coal from southern West Virginia mines to Tidewater at Norfolk in direct competition with the Norfolk & Western and Chesapeake & Ohio railways.

The Virginian was the last of the large (Class I) railways built in West Virginia and came very late in the era of new railroad construction. Because of this and because of its almost complete preoccupation with coal hauling, it did not have many of the normal characteristics of railroads built earlier and with a more diverse approach. It had a modest passenger service with its only through trains connecting first with C&O and later with NYC at Deepwater where they ran on trackage rights to Charleston. Its non-coal freight business was modest as well, with one set of "fast freight" trains that traversed the line, again ending with connections at Deepwater for through interline cars. It had no other through fast freight service. Virginian's local freight service was relatively small and accommodated what was normal for the various stations along its line.

In 1898, William N. Page, a businessman from Ansted, W. Va., purchased a short four-mile line that connected a lumber mill at Robson with the mainline of the Chesapeake & Ohio at Deepwater, a station along the Kanawha River in Fayette County. He incorporated the line as the Deepwater Railway, and leased it to the C&O for operation. Soon thereafter, he interested Henry Huddleston Rogers, who was a vice president of the Standard Oil Company, to invest in the Deepwater which would help fulfill Page's ambition to reach the blossoming coal fields. Failing to secure good rates for delivery of coal and lumber to the C&O and

N&W, Page and Rogers decided to extend their line all the way to the coast in competition with these two larger, well established lines.

To accomplish the eastward extension, the Tidewater Railway was incorporated in Virginia in 1904, while the Deepwater began construction eastbound in the West Virginia coal fields. In 1907 the Deepwater and Tidewater were merged to form the new Virginian Railway. Meanwhile, the Deepwater tracks had reached Mullens, which became the site of Virginian's large Elmore yard and later the hub of its electric operations (see below). During its expansion in the coal fields both N&W and C&O opposed it. C&O engaged in a very well publicized "war" with Deepwater construction forces in the Winding Gulf coal fields near Beckley, but the Virginian won out and as a result for many decades to come several of the mines in this region were jointly served by both C&O and Virginian.

By 1909 the Virginian main line had been completed to Norfolk, with its ocean terminal at Sewall's Point in that city. It was laid on a good gradient along the 400+ miles between the old Deepwater location and Hampton Roads.

Because Virginian was built late in the railway age it had the benefits of advanced construction and engineering techniques, but it was also restricted by a series of heavy grades on its main line in West Virginia, certainly as steep as N&W's line and much worse than C&O's. The most notable grade was a long 12-mile 2% grade from Elmore to Clarks Gap, just to the north of the N&W's Elkhorn grade, the heaviest on its line.

Just as Virginian was being created, the age of the large steam locomotive for heavy coal trains was opening in the form of the compound articulated or "Mallet" type. This was named for its Swiss inventor, Anatole Mallet and is pronounced "MAL-ay." These huge locomotives soon became the regular power for increasingly heavy coal trains on C&O, N&W and Virginian in the years from 1918 until the end of steam in 1955.

Opposite: One of the Virginian's best known operations was its electrified territory, extending all the way from Mullens, West Virginia to Roanoke, Virginia, about 136 miles, that included the region where the heaviest grades were encountered by eastbound coal trains. Beginning in 1925 and lasting until just after the N&W merger, Virginian electrics handled a huge amount of coal over this route. Here a set of the famous "Jack-Shaft" electrics, No. 105, takes a westbound over one of the high trestles near Oakvale, West Virginia, on June 13, 1956. (Richard J. Cook Photo)

Top: Typical of Virginian depots in West Virginia is Pax (photo taken about 1930), which served the Virginian mainline trains (track at left), and the local trains operated by the Kanawha, Glen Jean & Eastern, which ran from Pax to Glen Jean, where it connected with C&O. It was a coal short line that was later taken over by the C&O, but its coal originally went to both C&O and Virginian. All of Virginian's passenger business was local so there were no imposing stations. (Lloyd D. Lewis Collection)

Above: Another joint station built by the Virginian at Oak Hill, near the coal center of Beckley. This station served both the Virginian and the C&O by way of the White Oak Railroad, which was jointly owned by the two railways for a long while. The dark paint in this B&W photo (ca. 1930) was the Virginian's deep orange, with white trim, used on its stations in the period through the 1930s. (Lloyd D. Lewis Collection)

In 1909 Virginian purchased the first of a long line of Mallet types when it acquired a 2-6-6-0. This articulated locomotive convinced Virginian management that this was the type needed for its heavy coal trains on steep grades. As a result, over the next decade and a half, it acquired several groups of compound articulated types, including mainly 2-8-8-2s, but also some monster 2-10-10-2s, and a single unsuccessful 2-8-8-8-4. These locomotives handled Virginian's heavy coal business until 1925 when its mainline was fully electrified the 133.6 miles between Mullens, West Virginia and Roanoke, Virginia. From that time onward until the line was merged with N&W (in 1959) and the electrification removed in 1962, Virginian was an example of how electrification could positively affect steam railroad operations. Though neighbor N&W had an electrified section installed about a decade earlier on its heavy grades just to the south, it was not nearly as long as the Virginian's.

Virginian purchased 12 sets of 3-unit class EL-3A electric locomotives initially, and didn't add to the fleet until it got four streamlined EL-2B two-unit monsters in 1948. The last electrics, class EL-C, came in 1956-57, just before the merger with N&W and end of electric operations. All of these locomotives could move coal east in larger trains than steam locomotives and at least twice the speed of steam.

For its passenger trains, which were basically just local accommodations, Virginian had 4-6-2 Pacific types. Several classes of 2-8-2 Mikado types pulled the non-coal freight trains, and also handled the heavy switching work. A few 4-4-0s and 4-6-0s were inherited from early Deepwater and Tidewater operations, and the line also had some 0-6-0 and 0-8-0 switchers for yard work, some of which were bought used from the C&O. In 1945-46 the last new steam came to Virginian in the form of some 2-8-4 Berkshire types and the gargantuan 2-6-6-6 AG class, both of which were based directly on C&O designs. However, these locomotives seldom if ever ventured onto Virginian's West Virginia lines, since these areas were electrified during the entire life of these classes.

The Virginian's freight car fleet was largely the standard 50-ton hopper car for coal transportation since that was the line's main business. The C&O and N&W also had large hopper car fleets for their giant coal business from the same region, but they also had considerable general freight business whereas Virginian did not, therefore its fleet of box, flat, gondola, covered hopper, and other general freight cars was quite small.

Likewise, since it had little through passenger business and operated a small local passenger train fleet it had a very small fleet of passenger cars consisting almost completely of coaches and combination mail/express cars. The only through arrangement was at first with the C&O, which allowed Virginian passenger trains to use its line from Deepwater into West Virginia's capital city of Charleston and on to Ashland, Kentucky. After 1931 this service was changed over to the New York Central's line into Charleston (see below). As with all common carriers of the era, however, it did provide accommodation passenger trains for local business on its mainline and on its branches in the West Virginia coal fields.

Through the 1920s, both C&O and N&W remained interested in acquiring the Virginian, both to get access to the mines it served, and to eliminate it as competition. N&W made an attempt to lease the Virginian in 1925 but it was prevented from doing so by the Interstate Commerce Commission. The New York Central and Pennsylvania Railroads were also both interested in acquiring the Virginian in this era, but likewise were unsuccessful.

In 1931 Virginian completed a bridge across the Kanawha River at Deepwater and connected with the New York Central's Kanawha & Michigan line (see page 108), and thereafter ran through passenger trains over the K&M line into Charleston (instead of on C&O as it had done previously). Virginian also interchanged traffic with the NYC, giving it another avenue to ship coal westward. Some westbound coal was also shipped over C&O from the Virginian connection at Gilbert, W. Va., on C&O's Logan Branch, and with N&W.

Most Virginian branch line local passenger trains were discontinued by the early 1940s, while a small scale mainline service continued. Trains

Electrification

In the early years of the 20th Century, the idea of electrifying railroads came to the fore, and during the next decades some mainline steam-operated railroads in the U. S. were electrified, though the idea never caught on in this country. Many foreign lines were electrified during the 20th century and most of today's high speed trains overseas are electric. Electrification simply means that wires are strung over the rails and locomotives are built which don't have engines in them but just electric motors. Pantographs, which are large devices that extend from the roof of the locomotive up to the overhead electrical wires (called "catenaries'), draw electrical current from the wires which are used to turn the motors in the locomotive and propel the driving wheels. Power is supplied usually by a dedicated power plant owned and operated by the railroad, but electricity could be purchased from an outside generating company. Both N&W and Virginian, West Virginia's only electrified lines, had their own power plants.

into West Virginia from Roanoke were discontinued in 1955, and the operations east of Roanoke in 1956.

The Virginian dieselized using Fairbanks-Morse locomotives, and in fact it was the only Class I railroad to dieselize almost entirely with F-M locomotives. The 2,400-horsepower "Train Master" models were used in the coal fields, and smaller 1,600-horsepower F-M engines were used on the coal trains east of Roanoke. Since Virginian's electrics handled its heaviest mainline business, only a limited number of diesel units was needed to eliminate steam operations.

Finally, in 1959 N&W's desire to acquire the Virginian was fulfilled as it was given permission to merge the line, which was approved by the stockholders of both companies. One of N&W's first actions was to eliminate Virginian's electrification (which was gone by 1962), as it had done with its own in 1950. One of the major benefits of the merger was that N&W could use some of Virginian's better grades east of Roanoke, and also establish one-way traffic on the two mainlines for heavy coal business, taking advantage of the better grades of the Virginian for eastbound coal.

The Virginian station at Princeton stood for many years but was eventually demolished. Today the depot has been rebuilt using original plans, but just not to the same exact size, and it houses a new railroad museum devoted to the Virginian. The ugly dispatcher's office that stuck out toward the track has not been replicated! In this July 29, 1953 scene an MB class 2-8-2 is switching the yard, which is loaded with hopper cars that Virginian lettered so boldly. (H. Reid Photo)

Opposite Top: Mikado (2-8-2) type No. 443 is seen in this sharp engineer's side view at Princeton yard on July 26, 1949, where it is probably being used as the shop and yard switcher (note overhead wires). The MB class was the heaviest and most powerful of Virginian's five classes of Mikados (amounting to 41 of the 85 the road owned). It was built in 1910 and was used for general freight service and switching. (A. A. Theime photo)

Opposite Center: Virginia AD Class 2-8-8-2 No. 605, one of the world's largest locomotives when built, sits on the ready track at Elmore yard in the 1920s. Soon it will depart to push an eastbound "hill run," to the top of Clark's Gap or perhaps to gather cars from coal mines as a mine shifter. (Lloyd D. Lewis Collection)

Opposite Bottom: The biggest of four triplexes ever built, Virginian XA Class 2-8-8-8-4 No. 700 has her workings oiled by the seemingly small engineer in the foreground. This photo was taken shortly after the leased locomotive (Virginia never bought the giant from Baldwin Loco. Works) was put in service in January 1917. (Lloyd D. Lewis Collection)

Princeton was Virginian's principal shop town, located on the main line just before it passed into Virginia. The large passenger station and office building is seen in this August 1954 photo with No. 103-3 stopped to do some business with its usual light Pacific locomotive and three cars. (Jay Williams Collection)

USA Class 2-8-8-2 No. 704 in Elmore yard (near Mullens) is ready to leave on a mine shifter run to deliver empty cars to mines and pick up loads on August 9, 1948. Many others of Virginian's fleet of huge Mallets surround it on all sides. No. 704 was one of 20 2-8-8-2s built in 1919 for Virginian using World War I standards of the U. S. Railroad Administration (when railroads were government operated for three years), and in this photo it is still working hard thirty years later in the deep valleys of West Virginia. (H. Reid Photo, TLC Collection)

Another view of a USA-class, No. 710, shows the Elmore coaling station in the background. The air pumps mounted on the smoke box front were to allow the maximum boiler width given clearances. Because of numerous shoppings and modifications over time, the locomotive looks like a pipe fitter's nightmare. (H. Reid Photo, TLC Collection).

Here one of the USA-class 2-8-8-2s is seen at Princeton, just after emerging from Virginian's main locomotive shops in that West Virginia city, shining in new paint and ready to resume its dirty coal fields work in about 1949. (TLC Collection)

This photo taken in September 1950 at Elmore yard shows USE-class No. 736 about to head up the Virginian mainline to Deepwater and perhaps Dickinson, W. Va. (connection with the NYC), on a mine run. However, this locomotive is a bit unusual. It has "seen the country," so to speak. Originally built in 1919 as Y4 class for the Norfolk & Western, it and others were sold to power-strapped Santa Fe in 1943. They spent four years in New Mexico, Arizona, and California, then were sold to Virginian in 1947 where they ran out their lives in the familiar surroundings of Appalachian coal country, on their third railroad! (H. H. Harwood, Jr. Collection)

This 1930s photo shows the Mullens depot area with Train No. 14 at left (operating from Princeton up the Stone Coal and Winding Gulf Branches) and mainline local No. 3 at right with a Virginian business or parlor car on the rear. (TLC Collection)

Virginian cabooses abound at Elmore yard on July 27, 1948. Needed for the many main line and mine shifter runs that operated out of this central coal fields yard, the wooden cars were kept in top condition. As with many wooden cabooses, the cupolas are stabilized by rods with turnbuckles. After all, these cars received a lot of heavy use. (H. Reid Photo)

Virginian didn't have many switchers, but in September 1950 the road bought five excellent 0-8-0s from neighboring C&O, which was quickly dieselizing its switching operations at that time. They were fairly new, having been built by Lima Locomotive Works in 1942. Virginian put them to good use until 1956-57 when they were retired. Here No. 243 is working at Mullens on August 19, 1952. (A. A. Thieme, Jr. Photo)

At Bud, West Virginia, motor No. 103 takes a loaded train east consisting of regular hopper cars and a few of Virginian's huge (for the era) 100+ ton gondolas. (Lloyd D. Lewis Collection)

The jagged profile of the Virginian's electrified territory shows how heavy eastbound coal trains had to climb the Clarks Gap grade which was 2.11% at its steepest (2.11 feet climb per 100 feet traveled). (Lloyd D. Lewis collection)

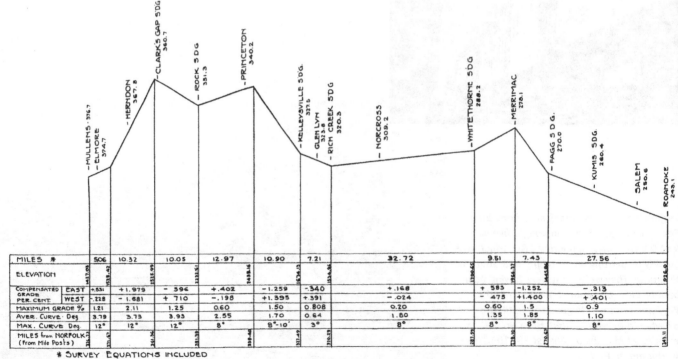

MILES *	506	10.32	10.05	12.97	10.90	7.21	32.72	9.51	7.43	27.56
ELEVATION										
COMPENSATED GRADE PER CENT — EAST	+.531	+1.979	-.396	+.402	-1.259	-.340	+.168	+.585	-1.252	-.313
COMPENSATED GRADE PER CENT — WEST	-.228	-1.681	+.710	-.198	+1.395	+.391	-.024	-.475	+1.400	+.401
MAXIMUM GRADE %	1.21	2.11	1.25	0.60	1.50	0.808	0.20	0.60	1.5	0.9
AVER. CURVE Deg.	3.79	3.73	3.93	2.55	1.70	0.64	1.80	1.35	1.85	1.10
MAX. CURVE Deg.	12°	12°	12°	8°	8°-10°	3°	8°	8°	8°	8°
MILES from NORFOLK (from Mile Posts)										

* SURVEY EQUATIONS INCLUDED

Condensed Profile of the Electrified Section

Covel, West Virginia, with its long curving trestle was always a favorite of Virginian photographers, and here No. 107 has an extra east of 28 loads at 10:23 a. m., June 14, 1950. In the town below workers apply a tar-paper roof to one of the houses. (Richard J. Cook Photo)

Westbound electric No. 101 is taking a long train of empties toward the coal fields, passing one of the streamlined EL-2B electrics that Virginian acquired in 1948 to supplement the old Jack-Shafts, at Kellysville, W. Va. at 4:25 pm June 10, 1949. (Richard J. Cook photo)

This nice portrait view of the lead unit of motor set No. 103 shows very well the utilitarian (and one might even say ugly) design of Virginian's EL-3A class electrics of the 1920s, with its pantograph folded at Mullens, May 18, 1954. (M. D. McCarter Collection)

The four class EL-2B electrics that General Electric built for Virginian in 1948 were, appropriately enough, known as "streamliners." These sleek looking, two-unit sets were so modern looking compared with the old box-cab electrics that they seemed to have come from a different world. Also note that their electric drive consisted of traction motors mounted on the axles, just like diesel-electrics, and unlike the hulking jack-shafts with their huge steam-like driving wheels. The 127 set is seen here at Mullens "Motor Barn," the base shop for electric locomotive maintenance at the west end of the electrified section in May 1953. (M. D. McCarter Collection)

The Mullens "Motor Barn" engine house serving the electric locomotives was a famous institution on the Virginian, and the structure still stands today, although it is no longer used. This June 18, 1949 photo shows the old box-cab and the new streamlined electrics. (Richard J. Cook Photo).

EL-2B No. 129, flying the while flags on an extra, heads eastward over the big curving trestle above the town of Covel in this 1949 photo. The train consists entirely of Virginian's hulking 100+ ton gondolas that could only be unloaded by rotary dumpers and therefore were captive to the coal-fields-to-Sewall's Point piers service. (George Shands Photo, L. D. Lewis Collection)

In 1956 Virginian received 12 Class EL-C electrics from GE, numbered 130-141. Still infants when the Virginian was merged in 1959 and the electrification abandoned within three years, they were sold to the New Haven Railroad, and later saw service in the Northeast on Penn Central and Conrail. Two are preserved in museums. Two are seen here at Tralee, as Clarks Gap pushers returning to Elmore yard in September 1958 (H. H. Harwood, Jr. Collection)

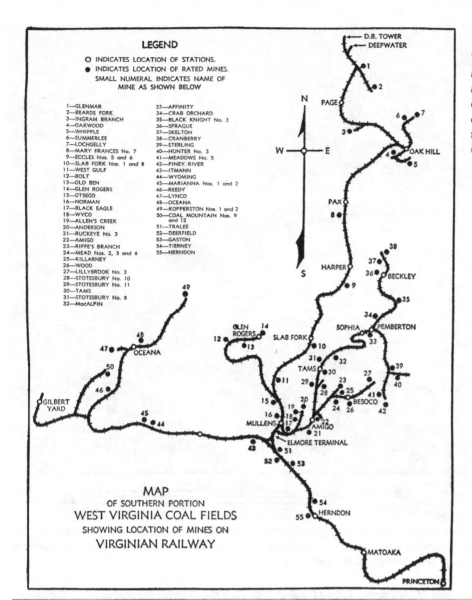

LEGEND

○ INDICATES LOCATION OF STATIONS.
● INDICATES LOCATION OF RATED MINES.
SMALL NUMERAL INDICATES NAME OF
MINE AS SHOWN BELOW

1—GLENMAR	33—AFFINITY
2—BEARDS FORK	34—CRAB ORCHARD
3—INGRAM BRANCH	35—BLACK KNIGHT No. 3
4—OAKWOOD	36—SPRAGUE
5—WHIPPLE	37—SKELTON
6—SUMMERLEE	38—CRANBERRY
7—LOCHGELLY	39—STERLING
8—MARY FRANCES No. 7	40—HUNTER No. 3
9—ECCLES Nos. 5 and 6	41—MEADOWS No. 5
10—SLAB FORK Nos. 1 and 8	42—PINEY RIVER
11—WEST GULF	43—ITMANN
12—BOLT	44—WYOMING
13—OLD BEN	45—MARIANNA Nos. 1 and 2
14—GLEN ROGERS	46—REEDY
15—OTSEGO	47—LYNCO
16—NORMAN	48—OCEANA
17—BLACK EAGLE	49—KOPPERSTON Nos. 1 and 2
18—WYCO	50—COAL MOUNTAIN Nos. 9 and 12
19—ALLEN'S CREEK	51—TRALEE
20—ANDERSON	52—DEERFIELD
21—BUCKEYE No. 3	53—GASTON
22—AMIGO	54—TIERNEY
23—RIFFE'S BRANCH	55—HERNDON
24—MEAD Nos. 2, 3 and 6	
25—KILLARNEY	
26—WOOD	
27—LILLYBROOK No. 3	
28—STOTESBURY No. 10	
29—STOTESBURY No. 11	
30—TAMS	
31—STOTESBURY No. 8	
32—MacALPIN	

MAP
OF SOUTHERN PORTION
WEST VIRGINIA COAL FIELDS
SHOWING LOCATION OF MINES ON
VIRGINIAN RAILWAY

This 1959 map depicts the locations and names of coal mines on the Virginian. As the map shows, Elmore yard at Mullens was the center for collection or marshalling of loaded coal headed east and west, and for the distribution of empty cars to the mines. (Lloyd D. Lewis Collection)

When the time arrived for Virginian to dieselize it didn't need a large fleet since the electrified territory handled most of the heaviest part of the line's traffic. Therefore, the road adopted the Fairbanks Morse Train Master 6-axle 2,400 horsepower units for the coal fields (Nos. 50-74) and a smaller 4-axle version for the easy grades east of Roanoke. Virginian was the only railroad to have an all F-M fleet (except for one other locomotive). Here No. 57 has a mine shifter replacing one of the line's big 2-8-8-2 steamers. (H. H. Harwood, Jr. Collection)

One of the brightly painted Train Master units handles another mine shifter near the mining town of Tams in about 1958. (Pat Dobbin photo, H. H. Harwood, Jr. collection)

This scene is at the Deerfield mine, one of the few located east of Mullens. The modern tipple is seen loading different grades of coal on six tracks into 50-ton Virginian hopper cars in 1950. (George Shands photo, Lloyd D. Lewis Collection)

Another typical mine scene is at Royal with a Trainmaster delivering empties to the tipple in April 1955 (Pat Dobbin, H. H. Harwood, Jr. Collection)

Squeezed in the valley in the Winding Gulf region, Tams was the archetype of a West Virginia coal town, with its tipples, company-owned houses, multiple railroad tracks, and community facilities such as the ever-present church (in the center distance). (Pat Dobbin photo, H. H. Harwood, Jr. Collection)

The very clean, modern looking Tierney mine tipple near Herndon, W. Va. off the mainline on the Clarks Gap grade is seen in 1953 with a variety of Virginian hopper cars including wooden composites and some just recently painted. (Pat Dobbin photo, Lloyd D. Lewis Collection)

VGN USA class 2-8-8-2 No. 718 on September 3, 1953, is pulling a train of empty hopper cars west at Surveyor, W. Va. It has just come out of Elmore yard at Mullens and will distribute the empties to mines along the main and branches to the west. (Richard J. Cook Photo)

Pacific type (4-6-2) No. 211 has three-car Virginian mainline train No. 4/104 in tow at Hamilton, just east of Page, a bit late, at 9:55 am, on June 12, 1950. It consists of a combination car with a short Railway Post Office space plus area for express and baggage, and two coaches. After the early 1930s, Virginian trains lacked such amenities as diners, lounges, and sleeping cars. No. 4/104 originated at Charleston (via trackage rights over the New York Central to Deepwater), at 7:55 a. m., reached Roanoke at 4:35 p.m., where its equipment then turned around the next morning as No. 3/103 leaving Roanoke at 7:30 a.m. and arriving Charleston at 4:25 pm. If one wanted to take the Virginian on to Norfolk an all-night layover was needed in Roanoke. Most folks transferred to N&W for the balance of that trip if desired. (Richard J. Cook Photo)

The three car No. 3-103 is speeding along the New York Central track east of Charleston in this 1944 photo with its accustomed Pacific type locomotive and three cars, even in the wartime year of 1944. (Glenn Grabill Jr. photo, H. H. Harwood, Jr. Collection)

Although the Virginian came only within 30 miles of West Virginia's capital, it reached there through trackage rights over New York Central and its passenger trains served the city. Here one is standing at the Charleston station while an NYC train sits to the right. (Thornton Wise Photo, TLC Collection)

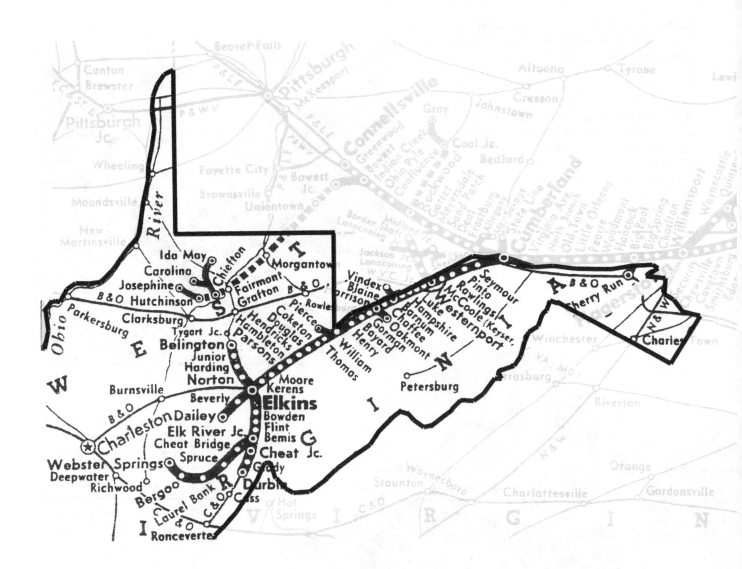

Western Maryland

The Western Maryland Railway (WM) operated lines in northeastern West Virginia, in territory close to Baltimore & Ohio operations in the same region of the state. WM's primary business was extracting coal and lumber.

Western Maryland traces it lineal descent from the Baltimore, Carroll & Frederick Rail Road, chartered in 1852, whose name was almost immediately changed to Western Maryland. It built a line from Baltimore toward the city of Hagerstown, Maryland. It reached Union Bridge, Maryland by 1862, however construction was interrupted by the War Between the States. The line finally reached Hagerstown in 1872. In 1881 WM acquired a line northward into Pennsylvania at Shippensburg where it obtained a through connection with the Reading Railroad. In 1886 it acquired a line to Gettysburg, Pennsylvania.

The WM main line entered West Virginia as it crossed the Potomac at Cherry Run, and connected with the B&O mainline, thence was built westward, crossing back into Maryland, to Cumberland (arriving there in 1906), another city served by B&O.

WM, as part of financier George Gould's railroad empire, then acquired the West Virginia Central & Pittsburg [sic] Railroad which had a line that skirted the Maryland/West Virginia border and then southwestward to Elkins, West Virginia, and from there to Durbin and Belington, deep in the state's great lumbering area, which also gave it access to coal fields around Elk Garden, Thomas, and Davis. Ridgely (on the West Virginia side of the Potomac, opposite Cumberland) and Elkins both became major operational points on the WM. In 1910 a line was built northwestward from Cumberland to Connellsville, Pa., where a connection was made with the Pittsburgh & Lake Erie and Pittsburgh & West Virginia, as well as the B&O. WM also had trackage rights over B&O from Con-

Opposite: Clean and shining, WM class H-8 2-8-0 No. 777 pulls a coal train out of Elkins, with a tank car tacked to the head-end on July 30, 1951. No. 777 was built in 1914 by Alco's Schenectady Works, and here is still hard at work 37 years later . . . but not for long as the end of steam was near. (TLC Collection)

nellsville into West Virginia, through Morgantown and Fairmont to reach WM-owned branches in the coal fields near that city.

In 1909 Western Maryland left the Gould camp through bankruptcy and passed into the hands of John D. Rockefeller. In the 1920s WM purchased the Greenbrier, Cheat & Elk Railroad from the West Virginia Pulp & Paper Company. This line originally had been built as part of WVP&P Company's huge lumbering operation, and ran from Cheat Junction to Bergoo. WM also acquired the West Virginia Midland, which connected Bergoo to Webster Springs.

Rockefeller sold his WM shares to B&O in 1927. Because of objections by other lines, the B&O ownership did not extend to operational control and the controlling interest of over 40% stock ownership was treated by B&O strictly as an investment.

The last expansion of the WM was in 1944 when it acquired the Cumberland & Pennsylvania, a short line coal originator out of Cumberland, which didn't touch West Virginia.

WM lines had some of the steepest Class I mainline railroad lines in the country in the coal and lumbering region centered around Elkins.

Western Maryland never operated a large fleet of passenger trains, but as with all railroads in the earlier period, had passenger operations on its main and branch lines, some of which persisted into the modern era. In 1950 its mainline trains operated only the short 87 miles between Baltimore and Hagerstown, but had through connections available at Baltimore to the North and South via the Pennsylvania Railroad and B&O, although no through cars were operated. Other trains operated from Hagerstown to Cumberland and Elkins, and from Elkins to Durbin connecting with C&O Greenbrier branch trains. In the steam era these were handled by light Pacific (4-6-2) types. Passenger service barely lasted to the diesel era, but American Locomotive Company diesel units usually handled the remaining trains. By 1957 the only service was a single set of trains from Cum-

Typical of an early West Virginia Central & Pittsburg [sic] locomotive is this classic Consolidation (2-8-0) type. The WVC&P was merged into WM in about 1905, and its lines comprised most of the WM in West Virginia. (TLC Collection)

The neat WM combination (freight and passenger) station at Parsons, shown here in 1917, was typical of its depots in the state. (TLC Collection)

The Elkins passenger station and office was at the center of WM operations in the state and is pictured here on a postcard of the 1912-era. (TLC Collection)

berland to Elkins and a mixed train (freight and passengers) from Elkins to Durbin. By 1959 only the mixed train was left, carrying a passenger now and again in the high mountains of northeastern West Virginia

The steam locomotive fleet of the Western

Maryland consisted of a core of ever larger 2-8-0 Consolidation types which it purchased through the 1920s. These were used on its heavy grades and coal trains, often in multiples. This was in stark contrast with B&O, N&W, and Virginian, which were using quantities of compound and simple articulated locomotives starting in 1910. However, not to be left behind in motive power development, WM did acquire some 2-6-6-2s compound articulateds in 1909, and some 2-8-8-2s a few years later. The best of the articulated types came in 1940-41 in the form of twelve 4-6-6-4 simple articulateds. Unlike the Mallets (see page 13) these locomotives didn't reuse steam, but all four cylinders were supplied with high-pressure steam directly from the boiler. Despite their advanced design they spent much of their time as pushers rather than the fast road engines they were intended to be. WM also had 30 2-10-0s, purchased in 1918 and 1927, the final 20 of which were giants, with nearly as much power as an articulated.

The last steam locomotives WM bought were powerful 4-8-4s in 1947 at the very end of commercial steam construction in the U. S. WM did, along with C&O, use Shay geared locomotives on some of its heaviest grades in the coal country of West Virginia and in 1945 bought the last Shay ever built which was also the largest three-truck Shay of all time. It was used until diesels took over its work in 1953. WM began to dieselize in 1950 and retired its last steam about five years later. Its black diesel paint scheme featured a red/white WM logo with wings behind it, implying speed, and was connected with a special font of lettering called "Speed Lettering," which was also meant to be modern and to impart a feeling of speed. Of course the speediest part of WM was its through freight business with the Reading at Shippensburg, Pa., while much its bread-and-butter business was slow coal trains out of the West Virginia fields. In fact, coal amounted for almost half of its revenues in the period discussed in this book.

One of WM's connections was with C&O's

Greenbrier branch at Durbin, West Virginia. In the 1920s C&O and WM established a fast freight line whereby through cars from the south and west were carried over the C&O and delivered to WM at Durbin, where they were taken onward to Hagerstown and a connection with the Pennsylvania Railroad which thus gave access to the Northeastern cities. This was a rather unlikely service given the mountainous country through which both lines operated, but it bypassed some major terminals further to the east and north and apparently was well used in the 1920s and into the 1930s. Otherwise, the C&O and WM's lines in this region had lumber and coal as their major originating traffic.

Over the years, as the forests were depleted the wood-product traffic dwindled on both lines.

Western Maryland continued its independent operation (although 40+% owned by B&O) until the merger era of the 1960s, at which time its management decided that it would fit best into the C&O/B&O system which had been created in the early 1960s. As a result, B&O was allowed to control the line after 1967. In 1975 it became part of the new Chessie System Railroads (consisting of C&O, B&O and WM). Today its remaining lines are a part of CSX Transportation, the successor of Chessie System.

All the coal hauling railroads that served West Virginia had large fleets of "hopper" cars. The actual designation was "hopper bottom gondola car," but they were universally known as "hoppers." Here a string of typical WM hoppers of the variety that had two bays (note the sloping doors) and carried 60 tons. The cars display the famous WM "Speed-Lettering" logo. These cars had just been delivered in January 1953. (WM Photo, TLC Collection)

Western Maryland had a large station and operations in Cumberland, but most of its yard and other facilities were across the Potomac at Ridgely, West Virginia. This track plan shows the yards in that area. (TLC Collection)

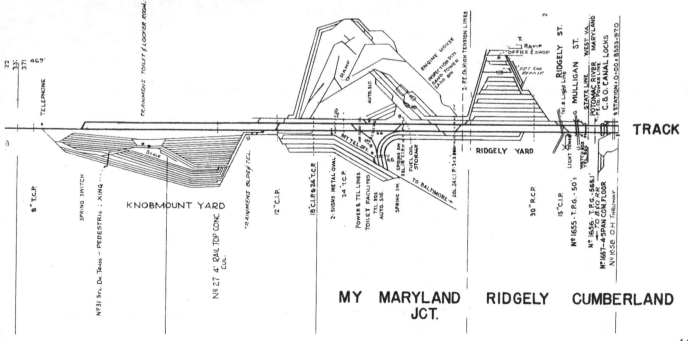

MY MARYLAND   RIDGELY   CUMBERLAND
JCT.

One of the most famous steam locomotives on WM was it giant Shay No. 6, which was used exclusively on the Chaffee Branch. Though the branch began at Chaffee, W. Va., most of the line and the mines were across the line in Maryland. Nonetheless, WM No. 6 has always been claimed as a West Virginia locomotive. Here it is at Vindex, Maryland, Aug. 19, 1946, soon after it arrived new from Lima Locomotive Works. (TLC Collection)

The big No. 6 Shay is seen here with a train of coal. The Shay remained in this service through 1953. Later it rested for many years at the B&O Railroad Museum in Baltimore, and today it is famous as one of the Shays operated on West Virginia's Cass Scenic Railroad State Park. (TLC Collection)

A profile of the Chaffee Branch shows why WM used Shays – the grade was far in excess of what railroads could normally accept. (TLC Collection)

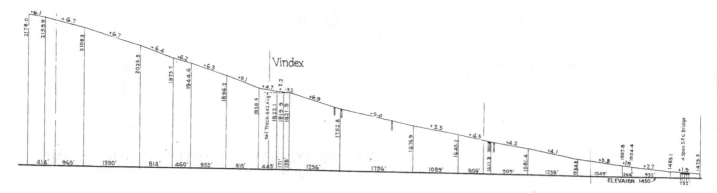

Shay No. 6 switching at Mauar Mine #1 near Vindex, Maryland on the Chaffee Branch in 1946. The branch connected with the WM mainline just across the boarder in West Virginia. (C.W. Jernstrom photo, TLC Collection)

Although the big Shay No. 6 got all the attention, publicity and interest, WM had four others (two of which were used into the 1940s and 1950s). No. 5 came to the railroad when it absorbed the Greenbrier Cheat & Elk, and was originally built for the Chesapeake and Ohio. Built in 1910 it was retired along with No 6, in 1953-54. This photo was taken at Ridgely in the 1940s. (Jay Williams Collection)

The short line Dry Fork Railroad connected with WM at Hendricks, W. Va., and in this 1906 photo the crude yard at that point is seen. The Dry Fork existed between 1895 and 1913. (TLC Collection)

A WM I-2 class 2-10-0 is ready for work at Ridgely in September 1949. Built in 1927, the big Decapod was ending over twenty years of heavy coal train work on WM. The 2-10-0 wheel arrangement was fairly uncommon in American railroading. (George Votava photo, TLC Collection)

WM 4-6-6-4 Challenger type simple articulated No. 1211 is on the ready track at Ridgely in September 1949. Locomotives of this type were usually for fast freight service, and though WM did use them that way, they were often assigned to pusher work and other slow freight activity that didn't fully utilize their potential. They were the only 4-6-6-4s ever operated regularly in West Virginia. (George Votava photo, TLC Collection)

Two of the giant WM challengers meet just west of Ridgely in the late 1940s in a superb company publicity photo which bespoke WM's high powered locomotive fleet. (WM Photo, TLC Collection)

At Elkins in 1913 we seen an ancient 4-4-0 American type in all its clean turn-of-the-century appearance on a WM passenger run. (TLC Collection)

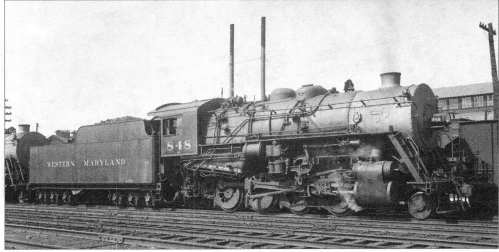

Perhaps the locomotive type for which WM is best remembered in its steam era is the 2-8-0 Consolidation type. Here No. 848 waits at Elkins terminal for its next coal hauling job on August 15, 1937. (TLC Collection)

This track chart gives an outline of tracks in the Elkins yard and terminal. Note the B&O connection going northwestward, and the line to Durbin running to the south. (TLC Collection)

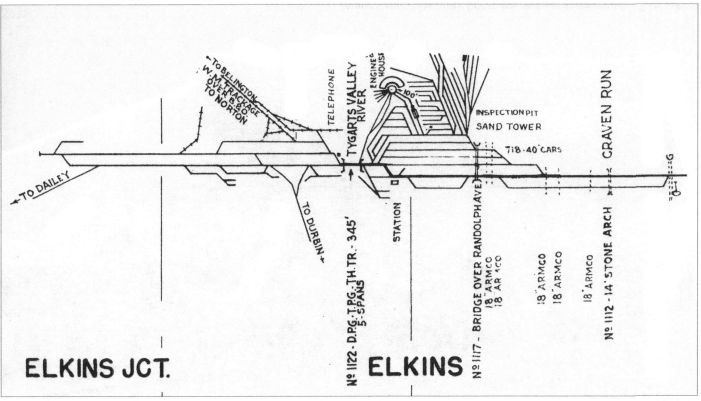

At the Elkins roundhouse in August 1937, we see 2-8-0 No. 456, one of four built for the line in 1903 by Baldwin Locomotive Works and classed H-4B by WM. The H-prefix was used for all the WM Consolidation types. This one had a long life, finding retirement in about 1948. (TLC Collection)

A superb photo shows WM Train No. 53 en route between Elkins and Durbin where it will connect with C&O's motor car train up from Ronceverte. Pacific type No. 153 has two wooden passenger cars in tow in this 1941 photo, having stopped for water in a rural setting on this line among the mountains of Randolph County. (Robert F. Collins photo)

Northeast of Elkins a WM freight is eastbound toward Cumberland in this photo from August 1968. The General Motors Electro-Motive GP-9 leads two products of the American Locomotive Company. WM bought a number of Alco diesels during its dieselization when that company still had a fair share of the diesel locomotive market. (A. D. Mastrogiuseppe photo, TLC Collection)

WM also had a small fleet of GM/EMD F7 road freight diesels. This late era photo from October 1975 shows No. 235 and mate with a train near Hendricks. In the early late 1960s, WM began painting its previously all-black diesels into a red/white/black scheme that many people called the "circus scheme." Of course soon after this photo most WM diesels that weren't retired got a Chessie System paint job. (Ron Piskor photo)

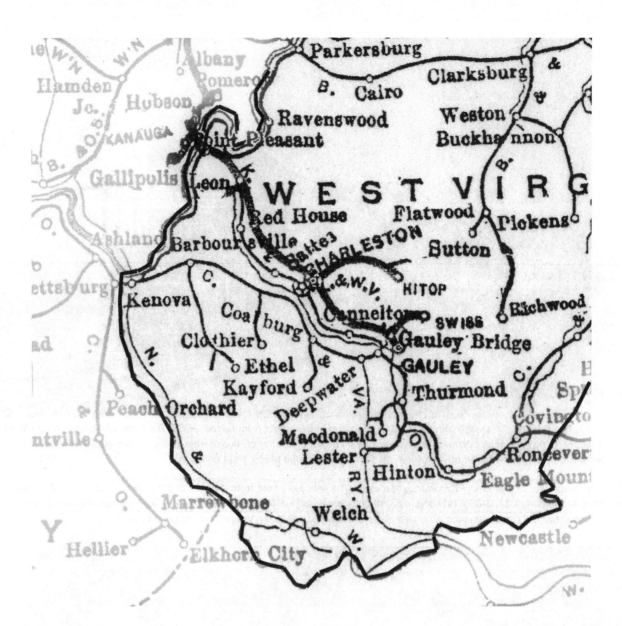

New York Central (Kanawha and Michigan)

The New York Central's entry into the West Virginia Coal Fields came in this way: After a number of false starts and a number of "paper railroads" projecting a line from Toledo to the coal fields of southeastern Ohio, the Ohio Central actually built a line extending from a connection with the Columbus, Hocking Valley & Toledo at Hobson, Ohio, thence across the Ohio River to Point Pleasant, West Virginia, and on to Charleston. It began operation in 1882. In 1884 a receivership caused a break-up of the line into the Toledo & Ohio Central (T&OC) and the Kanawha & Ohio Railways. The latter was reorganized in 1890 as the Kanawha & Michigan (K&M), taking over all the lines in West Virginia. However, the T&OC obtained control of the K&M in that year. After the turn of the 20th Century, Edwin Hawley, who was a railroad financial magnate, put together a group of railroads, including the Hocking Valley, the T&OC, and the K&M, using them in conjunction with the C&O which he also acquired, as an outlet not only for their own coal, but for westbound C&O coal from West Virginia. However, C&O was obliged to divest control of the T&OC and K&M in 1910, while retaining the HV, which later became an important link in its westbound coal trade. Meanwhile, NYC was able to obtain control of T&OC (which controlled K&M), and thus access to the Kanawha coal field of West Virginia and began leasing and operating the K&M in 1922. The K&M also controlled the Kanawha & West Virginia Railroad which was a short line from Charleston to Hitop, about 34 miles, plus a 9-½-mile branch.

As explained above, in the era of this book's coverage the mighty New York Central, one of the nation's largest railroads both in route miles and in freight and passenger traffic hauled, penetrated West Virginia through its K&M subsidiary. The NYC's lines also included the Nicholas, Fayette & Greenbrier (NF&G) Railroad, with it jointly owned with C&O. East of Charleston the K&M line featured numerous coal mines. From Gauley Bridge a branch connected with the NF&G which hauled coal from mines served principally by the NYC and some that were served jointly by NYC and C&O. Numerous mines were also located on this Gauley Branch. The short line Campbell's Creek Railroad served three mines east of Charleston, connecting with the NYC line near Malden. It was owned by the Hatfield-Campbell Creek Coal Company.

The Campbell's Creek Railroad had been incorporated in 1881 and was in operation by 1883 hauling coal for dumping into river traffic. It found railroad outlet in 1893 when the K&M purchased the Charleston & Gauley Railroad and finished its connection to the American railroad network. This decreased Campbell Creek's reliance on river shipping. The line was only about three miles in length, but to reach coal further from the river it expanded in 1901-02 about 12 miles, to Putney where new mines were opened. The railroad eventually reached about 14 miles in length and transported coal from about a dozen mines.

Additionally, the Kelley's Creek and Northwestern (6.5 miles) shortline served six mines and connected with the NYC at Warner. The KC&NW was owned by the Kelley's Creek Colliery Company to serve its mines.

Coal from the Kanawha field flowed westward to NYC lines in Ohio for general distribution in the Midwest.

It should be noted also that the NYC had a joint interest (through its Pittsburgh & Lake Erie Railroad subsidiary) with the Pennsylvania Railroad and the B&O in the Monongahela Railway of southern Pennsylvania and northern West Virginia, which served many mines in the B&O coal area. Its mainline ran from Brownsville Junction, Pa., to Fairmont, West Virginia, a distance of about 70 miles, and operated branches that aggregated about another 33 miles, and leased another 18 miles of branch lines (see page 23).

Opposite: Handsome NYC Pacific type (4-6-2) No. 4905 is on one of the NYC passenger trains serving Charleston in this photo at that point taken August 11, 1935. (TLC Collection)

Kanawha and Michigan Railroad, Charleston, W.Va.

The large brick passenger station and office building at Charleston was a fitting gateway for the Kanawha & Michigan in the state capital. As shown in this ca. 1915 postcard, its architecture was similar to that used on other K&M and T&OC depots in Columbus and other Ohio locations. A light 4-4-0 American type is seen on the has the local passenger train between Charleston and Columbus. This station was located on the north side of the Kanawha River in the main part of Charleston. (TLC Collection)

To handle yard work and to switch industries in the highly industrialized city of Charleston, NYC used this neat looking 0-8-0 switcher No. 7760 shown in Charleston in 1935. (William Monypeny photo, TLC Collection)

Much of NYC's business in West Virginia was hauling coal westward and strong-looking Mikado (2-8-2) types such as No. 9707 shown here, were an important part of the motive power fleet used in that service. It is pictured at Dickinson yard, about 13 miles east of Charleston. (William Monypeny Photo, TLC Collection)

Unusual was a NYC 2-8-2 "Tank" locomotives that was headquartered at Dickinson yard, where it did heavy switching work. It was unusual for major railroads to employ tank locomotives. Dickinson remains an important yard today on the former NYC line now operated by Norfolk Southern. Tank locomotives carried their water and coal on the engine rather than an attached tender. (TLC Collection)

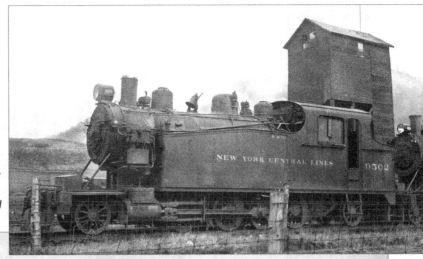

This neat little 4-4-0 was built by American Locomotive Company for the Kanawha & West Virginia, which became part of the K&M in 1922 when the NYC assumed control of both. (TLC Collection)

In this photo taken August 11, 1935, Kelley's Creek & Northwestern 2-8-0 Consolidation No. 6 is switching coal cars which will eventually make their way down to the NYC (K&M) mainline and on to Midwestern markets. The KC&NW was wholly owned by the Kelley's Creek Colliery Company to move coal from its mines along the 6-½-mile line. It was a Class III common carrier railroad. (TLC Collection)

Campbell's Creek Railroad was a common-carrier Class III line owned by the Hatfield-Campbell's Creek Coal Company and successors. It operated four locomotives, including this good-looking 2-8-0 Consolidation type, to handle business on the 13.8 mile line taking coal to the NYC line at Dana. (TLC collection)

This nice photo of a sparkling clean W&LE 2-8-2 Mikado is at the W&LE terminal in Wheeling in January 1935. (TLC Collection)

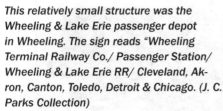

This relatively small structure was the Wheeling & Lake Erie passenger depot in Wheeling. The sign reads "Wheeling Terminal Railway Co./ Passenger Station/ Wheeling & Lake Erie RR/ Cleveland, Akron, Canton, Toledo, Detroit & Chicago. (J. C. Parks Collection)

This is Pennsylvania Railroad Train No. 701 at Wheeling in 1949. It consisted of a motor car/coach for power, a sleeping car and a combination car. The heavyweight 8-section/4-double-bedroom sleeper originated in New York and was dropped by Train No. 67 (The American, operating New York - St. Louis) at Weirton Junction, West Virginia, where it was added to local motor train No. 701 for the 24.4-mile trip down the branch to Wheeling, arriving there at 7:35 a. m. It returned at 6:15 p.m. on No. 702 for a reverse move to New York via Train 16/38 from Weirton Junction. In 1949, Nos. 701 and 702 were the only PRR passenger service in the state. They were gone by 1956. (Bob Withers Collection)

P&WV acquired some large powerful simple articulated 2-6-6-4s such as No. 110 seen here at Pittsburgh. These locomotives served the line well as it hauled big trains of through freight while it was a key link in the "Alphabet Route" through freight arrangement of the 1930s-40s. Before the new 2-6-6-4s arrived from Baldwin Locomotive Works in 1935, P&WV's traffic was handled by twenty-two 2-8-0 and 2-8-2 types. (H.K. Volrath Collection)

Railroads in the Northern Panhandle

Three Railroads that had no other operations in West Virginia passed through the state's odd narrow Northern Panhandle, the Pennsylvania, Wheeling & Lake Erie, and Pittsburgh & West Virginia.

Pennsylvania Railroad

The giant Pennsylvania Railroad, whose lines crisscrossed Pennsylvania and Ohio, came into West Virginia only in the state's very narrow Northern Panhandle. The Northern Panhandle neck of land is created by West Virginia's Ohio River boundary on the west and on the east by Pennsylvania's straight line western boundary. The northern extremity of the panhandle reaches north of Pittsburgh geographically. The Pennsylvania Railroad's line between Pittsburgh and Columbus passed east-west through the Panhandle about 25 miles north of Wheeling. The line was intersected by a PRR branch than ran north-south along the West Virginia side of the Ohio River between Wheeling and Chester, which was a station at the very tip of the Panhandle. This line ran about 25 miles north of Weirton Junction to Chester and about the same distance south to Wheeling. Its obvious purpose was to enable the PRR to get its share of business from the Weirton and Wheeling steel mills. Except for the coal fields served by the Monongahela Railway (see page 23) in which PRR was a $1/3$ owner, the giant railroad had no other direct West Virginia operations.

Wheeling & Lake Erie Railroad

The Wheeling & Lake Erie was first organized in 1871 to build a line from Martins Ferry, Ohio, across the river from Wheeling, to Lake Erie. Construction started as a narrow gauge line in Norwalk, Ohio, in 1877, and after reorganization and gauge change finally reached Wheeling in 1891. The four miles between Wheeling at Martin's Ferry constituted the only W&LE trackage in West Virginia. It was primarily an Ohio coal hauler and later was important in automobile traffic, with lines to Zanesville, Harmon, Canton, Cleveland, Huron and Toledo. – It ran passenger trains to Wheeling until it gave up all passenger service in 1938. In 1948 W&LE operated 506 miles of road and was under the control of the Nickel Plate Road. After many mergers and reorganizations, some of its line is operated now by a new W&LE. A West Virginia road mainly by name, its trains did visit the sate, and from its Wheeling connection it did carry West Virginia coal to Lake Erie.

Pittsburgh & West Virginia

Another railroad that West Virginia in its name, but barely touched the state was the Pittsburgh & West Virginia Railway running in an almost straight 60-mile long east-west line from Pittsburgh to Pittsburgh Junction on the Wheeling & Lake Erie and Erie railroads and the W&LE near Hopedale, Ohio. The P&WV was a classic "connecting line" with few branches or any appreciable on-line business. Most of its traffic was to and from connecting railroads that it intersected. It was built in 1904 by George Gould when he was trying to establish a bridge for his W&LE and Wabash systems into Pittsburgh as the Wabash Pittsburg Terminal Railway. After the Gould bankruptcy, the line was reincorporated a the Pittsburgh & West Virginia in 1920. An extension of the line southeastward to Connellsville, Pennsylvania, was completed in 1931. This accomplished further connections with B&O and Western Maryland. In about 1930 the line was acquired by a subsidiary of the Pennsylvania Railroad which turned it into a profitable bridge line for east-west traffic. When N&W acquired the Nickel Plate Road and W&LE in 1964 it leased the P&WV. In about 1990 the new Norfolk Southern sold remaining portions of the W&LE and the lease for the P&WV to a new W&LE short line operator. – The P&WV passed through the very narrow Northern Panhandle of West Virginia with five stations within the state: Virginia, Cliftonville, Louise, Rockdale, and Wellsburg. At Wellsburg it connected with the PRR branch running along the West Virginia side of the Ohio River. Heavy coal traffic was also an important part of the P&WV business.

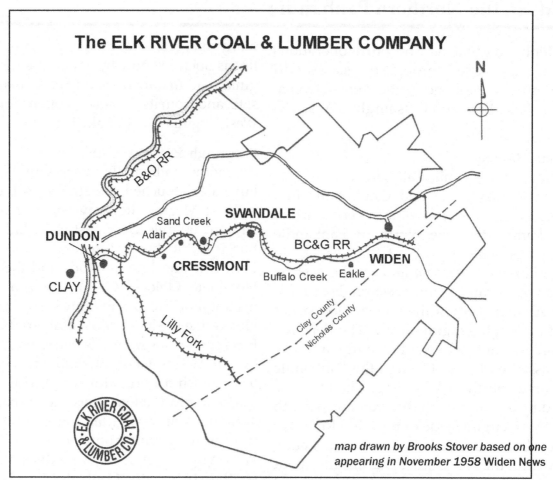

The ELK RIVER COAL & LUMBER COMPANY

N

B&O RR

SWANDALE

Sand Creek

DUNDON

Adair

BC&G RR

CRESSMONT

WIDEN

CLAY

Buffalo Creek

Eakle

Lilly Fork

Clay County

Nicholas County

ELK RIVER COAL & LUMBER CO.

map drawn by Brooks Stover based on one appearing in November 1958 Widen News

Short Lines

At the height of the railway age from 1870 to 1950, numerous short line railroads were built in all parts of the country. These lines sometimes served a particular need or were just a local feeder, funneling traffic to a bigger railroad. Many of these lines were ultimately merged into the larger systems, but some retained their independence into the more modern era of the 1930s-1950s. West Virginia had numerous short lines, most of which either were subsumed into larger railroads or simply went out of business when the commodity they were built to haul was exhausted or traffic patterns changed. This book makes no attempt to chronicle or list the many short lines of the state, but to give a sampling of the operations of a few which may serve as exemplar of the whole.

Several of the short lines that primarily funneled coal and lumber products to major railroads are treated with those railroads and don't appear here (see chapters on B&O, C&O, and NYC).

One of the most famous of the West Virginia short lines was in fact one of these, which for all intents and purposes acted as a branch of the Baltimore & Ohio, but because it lasted so long using steam locomotives, it received a great deal of attention from photographers, railfans, and historians, that is the Buffalo Creek & Gauley. For that reason this material is presented as an example of a successful short line feeder railroad in West Virginia.

Another line of similar dimension on the C&O was, and in this case is, the Winifrede Railroad, still in operation.

A third major short line is the Monongahela, but it is included in the B&O section, since it served essentially as a coal branch of the B&O (as well as the Pennsylvania Railroad and Pittsburgh & Lake Erie, since it was joint operation). Similar to it was the Nicholas, Fayette & Greenbrier, which served

Opposite: The reason for the BC&G: Elk River Coal & Lumber Company's Rich Run Mine at Widen is seen here with two BC&G locomotives shifting B&O hopper cars under the tipple in the 1940s. (Jay Williams Collection)

as a coal branch road for its joint owners C&O and NYC. The C&O pulled far more coal from it than NYC and also had the large lumber business from Meadow River Company's huge mill, so it has been treated in the C&O chapter.

Buffalo Creek & Gauley Railroad

The Buffalo Creek & Gauley began its life in April 4, 1904 with the original intent to build a 110-mile line from Dundon to Huntersville, West Virginia. It was, however, a wholly owned subsidiary of the Elk River Coal & Lumber Company which had mines and sawmills along its line. Though chartered with a grand vision, it only built 18.6 miles from Dundon, near the small town of Clay, to Widen, reaching the latter point in 1911 just as the large Rich Run Mine was opened. The big sawmill was at Swandale, about half-way along the line. The BC&G had about six miles of sidings and a half a mile of second (double) track. *Moody's Railroad Manual* of 1930 listed it as owning two locomotives, two passenger cars, six general freight and service cars, and 900 hopper cars.

Dundon is located in Clay County and is opposite the town of Clay. About a mile west of Dundon the BC&G interchanged first with the old Coal and Coke Railroad, and later with B&O after its 1917 takeover of the C&C.

By the 1950s sixty-to-eighty hopper cars of coal per day were being interchanged with B&O after coming down the BC&G from the end of its line at Widen (Rich Run Mine). In 1960 BC&G was still running steam locomotives and carrying about a million tons of coal a year. By this time all Class I railroads in the U. S. were totally dieselized, and BC&G became an oddity that attracted national attention from the curious and from thousands of railfans interested in this last remnant of fairly big-time steam railroading.

In its life, BC&G bought one new locomotive, its No. 4 (built by Baldwin Locomotive Works), and two of its sturdy 2-8-0s came second hand from Kelley's Creek & Northwestern in 1950. The Elk River Coal & Lumber's logging railroad, which connected with BC&G, had three Climax geared logging locomotives, as well as several Shays.

In 1959 the ERC&L Company was sold to Clinchfield Coal Company, which sold the sawmill and logging railroad to W. M. Ritter Lumber Company. Ritter continued the steam logging operation for a time. In 1963 the Rich Run Mine closed and the BC&G continued to operate only to haul lumber from the Swandale mill until early 1965. A small diesel switcher continued hauling lumber from Swandale until the mill finally closed in 1968. From time to time since then portions of the line have been open for short periods for various reasons.

The Winifrede Railroad

The Winifrede Railroad began its life as what might be called a "tram railroad" with rails consisting of wooden stringers having strap iron nailed to their tops, and oxen for motive power. It used crude four-wheel cars to move coal from the mine downgrade to the Kanawha River, starting in 1853, fully 20 years before the Chesapeake & Ohio's mainline would come by its line, and a dozen years before West Virginia was even a state. The down-grade gravity operation required only a brakeman riding and controlling by handbrake one of the cars, while the oxen hauled the empties back to the mine, seven miles away from the river. Most of the coal from the Winifrede mine was used by the salt furnaces which constituted the earliest industrial development in the region. At some point a steam locomotive was delivered by river barge and the Winifrede was a "real" railroad. Even the single car passenger train would be pulled up the mine by the locomotive and then would go back by gravity and braking. Not a very safe operation. Although much of Winifrede's coal was used locally, some seems to have found its way down the Kanawha and Ohio to Cincinnati by barge.

In 1861, at the outset of the War Between the States, the Winifrede Coal and Manufacturing Company was disbanded. It was not until 1881 that the Company was reorganized and operations began anew. The new Winifrede Railroad was incorporated in 1881 with the single purpose of taking coal from the Winifrede Coal Company to the Kanawha and the C&O at Winifrede Junction where C&O maintained an agent to handle coal originating on the short line. However, Winifrede continued to ship the bulk of its traffic via barge on the Kanawha River, and today still does that. Commercial navigation of the Kanawha as far as the falls was in operation in the late 1700s, and after 1820, when the James River & Kanawha Company took over water-way operation on the river, there was steady drumbeat for improvements. Eventually these occurred beginning right after the War Between the States and have been enlarged over the decades up until the present time. In the late 19th and through the 20th Centuries the Kanawha has proven to be a great route for carrying the raw materials of West Virginia: coal, lumber, salt, and farm products in the early days, then products of chemical plants, petroleum, etc., as well as coal in later times. Today the river con-

BC&G 2-8-0 No. 13 with empties is at Dundon heading for the Widen mine in December 1963 in the very last days of the operation. (Bob's Photo Collection)

tinues as a great avenue for coal transportation.

In the 1940s and 1950s the Winifrede operated steam locomotives purchased second-hand from C&O. It was later dieselized. In the 20th Century, it owned and operated about 60-80 coal hopper cars.

This classic Brill rail bus was what passed for passenger service on the BC&G, although in earlier times the line did have a regular passenger car. This photo was taken at Swandale, site of the big lumber mill, in 1963, again toward the last days of the BC&G when there were so many railfans visiting the line. (Bob's Photo Collection)

Here is Winifrede RR No. 9 under the brand new bridge of the West Virginia Turnpike (Now I-77) near Winifrede Junction about 1954. The locomotive was a former C&O class G-7 2-8-0 sold to the Winifrede in 1931. (Jay Williams Collection)

No. 8, another of the ex-C&O G-7 Consolidation types backs some side dump WRR hoppers at Winifrede Junction in the summer of 1954. (C&O Ry. Photo, C&OHS Collection)

Below Left: Archetype of the steam engineer in every particular, J. L. Osborne had been engineer on the Winifrede for eight years when this summer of 1954 photo was taken. He had worked as a C&O engineer out of Hinton for years before that. Note the C&O numbers under layers of paint on the cab side. (C&O Ry. Photo, C&OHS Collection)

This was the WRR engine house, water tank, and "yard" at Winifrede Junction, in the 1960s. The enginehouse still stands and is used by the present operators. (Larry Fellure Photo, Bob Withers Collection)

Logging Railroads

Although West Virginia has been most closely identified with its vast reserves of high grade bituminous coal, it was also once a great source of lumber and forest products from its huge virgin forests. In the 19th Century, long before the coming of the logging motor-truck used today, logs were dragged from the woods using horses and mules, and rafted down rivers and streams. The very act of getting them to the sawmills, even when those were located close to the woods, was one of the most expensive, dangerous, and arduous parts of the process.

Some early mills were supplied by logs floated down rivers in giant rafts. This was practical only if a stream of sufficient volume were available, and was dependent on the weather and flow of the river. It was also a dangerous and difficult operation to float huge logs down a river for many miles. An large early mill using this method was the St. Lawrence Boom & Lumber Company at Ronceverte. Its logs came down the Greenbrier River, and were caught in a huge "boom" that extended out into the river.

The tram road was another way that logs could be taken to the mill, but it was practical only for fairly short distances. In this method, logs were used as cross ties, and then planks were nailed to the top to accommodate the wheels of wagons. More boards were laid in the center for horses or mules to walk on. Each wagon had to have a driver and a brakeman, as grades were often steep. Although easy to build with the readily available logs and lumber, they could be used only short distances and in terrain that was generally favorable.

Opposite Top: A typical log train has just arrived at the Elk River Coal & Lumber Company mill at Swandale in the 1950s, with Shay No. 12, a four-wheel "bobber" caboose, four loaded log flats, and the log loader on the rear. (John Krause Photo, TLC Collection)

Opposite Bottom: This scene on Elk River Coal & Lumber Company's land on Lily Fork in the 1950s was typical of how logging railroads were laid and re-laid with crude log cross-ties, light rail, and little or no roadway preparation. Men in the background are using a track gauge to make sure the rails are exactly 4-feet, 8-½-inches apart. That was one thing that had to be right! (John Krause Photo, TLC Collection)

As lumber companies began to exploit timber from the deep woods, far distant from their mills, a better solution was needed. The use of railroads was, of course, logical given available technology. It was possible in some logging areas, such as Michigan where the terrain was essentially flat, to use small conventional rod locomotives. However, in mountainous regions such as West Virginia and the Pacific Northwest of the U. S., the rod locomotives simply would not meet the need of taking the logs from the woods to the mills.

Ephraim Shay, a Michigan area logger and inventor was the man who met this need with his creation of a "geared" steam locomotive. In his design the cylinders were arranged perpendicular to the track. They turned a drive shaft on the right side of the locomotive which was then attached to gears which powered the driving wheels of the locomotive. Instead of having large drivers they were small and mounted in bogie trucks, as on a freight cars. The geared drive shaft extended to all wheels under the locomotive, thus using all its weight to supply tractive effort. This ungainly locomotive was thus able to transmit great traction for hauling loads over grades that a rod engines could never accomplish. Since it had a short rigid wheelbase (just the length between two sets of wheels in a bogie truck) it could negotiate the sharpest of curves. It was also quite flexible and operated at low speeds, so the roadbed didn't have to be very smooth or well-built. Indeed, most logging roads were laid in the crudest possible way, and were often taken up and moved around in the woods as the trees in a particular area were exhausted.

As a result of Shay's work, his locomotive and two other geared types, the Climax and the Heisler, became standard in logging operations around the country and in West Virginia. The Shays with their offset boiler and two or three cylinders mounted on one side, were the most common type in the state. Heislers had two cylinders in a "V" shape under the boiler diving a central geared drive shaft. Climaxes had a cylinder on each side of the boiler in the usual rod-locomotive position, but they drove a universal gear under

119

The band saw was the invention that really changed logging into a high production industry. Replacing the much slower and less efficient circular saw, band mills predominated in West Virginia logging. This scene is at the Commonwealth Lumber Company's mill at Glenray, W. Va. about 1910 as the giant bands are being sharpened. (TLC Collection)

the boiler which in turn drove the geared wheels.

According to the definitive book on West Virginia logging, *Tumult on the Mountain*, there were about 130 Shays used on logging railroads in the state and about the same number of Climaxes, but only 13 Heislers. Although the number of Climax types was about the same as the Shays in West Virginia, nationally the Shay was by far the most popular of the geared logging locomotives. The Climax types also tended to be smaller/lighter than the Shays.

These geared locomotives were sturdy and could be maintained by the machine shops that were available at almost every large lumbering operation, and they were often traded or sold among companies. Few logging railroads lasted into the modern era, because eventually much of the work could be assumed by Caterpillar tractors and motor-trucks operating over lightly graded roads, so diesel locomotives never really had a chance to replace the geared steamers on logging railroads. One West Virginia logging line, Meadow River Lumber Company at Rainelle, did last well into the 1960s, and in its later years used small diesels to replace its geared locomotives. Some of the steamers also lasted into the 1960s as well.

West Virginia is fortunate today to have several tourist railroad operations, one of which, the Cass Scenic Railroad (which is operates as a state park), runs a sizeable fleet of Shay locomotives and one Heisler locomotive along a portion of the old Mower Lumber Company logging railroad. It has been one of the state's major attractions since its creation in the early 1960s. At least one Climax is also in operation on a nearby tourist line as well, out of Durbin. The Cass line also owns a Climax and it is hoped that one day it will become operational.

No accounting has yet been made or researched that has begun to chronicle all the many logging railroads in West Virginia, though many are covered extremely well in *Tumult on the Mountain* (McClain Printing Co., Parsons, W. Va.) and the five biggest which were also the last are covered in *West Virginia Logging Railroads* (TLC Publishing, Lynchburg, Va.)

It's interesting to note that two of West Virginia's Class I railroads, C&O and WM, also operated Shays within the state. C&O had a fleet of 16 huge Shays, including the heaviest ever built, which were used on several of its coal branches that had very steep grades. Western Maryland had a smaller fleet of Shays, but it included the largest 3-truck Shay ever built (which was also the last Shay ever built) on one of its steepest lines. Only a handful of other large American railroads besides these ever owned Shays. C&O sold its Shays in the 1920s, the last one being taken out of service in 1928. Two of them were sold to the W. Va. Pulp & Paper Co.'s Cass operation, and one of these was subsequently sold to the WM. Both were long ago scrapped. Western Maryland No. 6, the last Shay, worked until 1953 and is today in operation at the Cass Scenic Railroad.

When West Virginia was first opened to exploration and development, huge virgin forests of chestnut, oak, tulip poplar, hickory, walnut, and pine stretched out as far as the eye could see along the mountain ridges and vistas. At the higher elevations there was the sugar maple and the very valuable spruce.

As early as the 1770s crude water-powered saw mills were supplying lumber and wood products for local consumption and for export to the eastern portions of Virginia, mostly equipped with sash-saws. These early mills could produce perhaps 500 board-feet of lumber per day verses 100 for two strong men using a two-handled whipsaw. A board foot is the standard measurement of lumber and is represented by a slab of wood one foot by one foot by one inch thick. As time passed, the early mills were improved with multiple-bladed gang-saws, and, of course, steam replaced water as the primary power for the mills. By the 1880s large circular saws were employed in these mills further increasing their efficiency and production.

The final improvement to the saw mill was the employment of the band saw. First used in America in 1835, the band saw consisted of a single flexible steel band ranging from 10-16 inches wide and 35-45 feet long. It ran continuously over powered wheels with diameters of 5-11 feet. This allowed logs of any size to be cut and also reduced the amount of wood that was lost to saw dust as a result of the cutting of the blade. Keeping the saw teeth sharp was one of the larger efforts in the band mill operation. At the height of the logging era in West Virginia about 250 band mills were in operation. In 1880 302,000,000 board-feet of lumber was cut in West Virginia, and by 1909 this number had swelled to a billion and a half. By 1963, though, it was down to 445,000,000.

By 1907 a large percentage of the virgin forests had been cut. After that date there was a steady decline in the amount of lumber produced in the state, and therefore the number of logging railroads. By 1950 there were just a few large sawmills with extensive logging railroads still in operation. But, these persisted up to about 1960, allowing photographers, who were, by that time, interested in recording this industry to travel to the woods and take many of the photos that we have available today.

Elk River Coal & Lumber's Climax is fording Lily Fork in this 1957 photo, with a single flat and some supplies. Many times rails would simply be laid in a shallow stream. Logging lines didn't want to spend resources on trestles for their usually temporary lines. (John Krause Photo, TLC Collection)

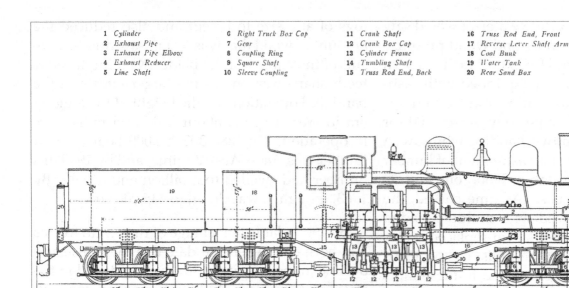

1	Cylinder	6	Right Truck Box Cap	11	Crank Shaft	16	Truss Rod End, Front
2	Exhaust Pipe	7	Gear	12	Crank Box Cap	17	Reverse Lever Shaft Arm
3	Exhaust Pipe Elbow	8	Coupling Ring	13	Cylinder Frame	18	Coal Bunk
4	Exhaust Reducer	9	Square Shaft	14	Tumbling Shaft	19	Water Tank
5	Line Shaft	10	Sleeve Coupling	15	Truss Rod End, Back	20	Rear Sand Box

This diagram shows the right side of a Shay geared locomotive, with the three perpendicular cylinders connected to the flexible drive shaft. As can be seen, even the water tender was used as tractive weight. (TLC Collection)

As this frontal photo illustrates, the Shay had an odd unbalanced look with the boiler offset to one side and all the external working parts on the other. This is F. C. Cook Lumber Company No. 16 at Alexander, W. Va. in the 1950s. (John Krause photo, TLC Collection)

This illustration shows the arrangement of the Climax type geared locomotive, which was almost equal to Shays in popularity on West Virginia logging lines. The cylinders were located on each side of the boiler set at an angle. They powered a central gearing that ran the drive shaft extending to the power trucks. (TLC Collection)

Elk River Coal & Lumber Company's Climax No. 3 is pictured at Dundon, W. Va., in the Spring of 1955. Note the external spark-arrester screening. This device was usually located inside a "Diamond" stack arrangement. (Charles E. Winters Collection)

This drawing illustrates a Heisler type geared logging locomotive. Note the cylinders are located under the boiler in a "V' shape, powering the drive shaft running beneath the locomotive. (TLC Collection)

Pardee & Curtin Lumber Company's No. 8 Heisler works the mill yard at Bergoo, where Western Maryland took the finished lumber to market. (William Monypeny, TLC Collection)

In a typical West Virginia logging railroad scene, Ely-Thomas Lumber Company Shay No. 3 in the mill yard at Fenwick, W. Va. The log loader is unloading logs to the pile at right. At left is finished lumber awaiting shipment, while the mill is to the right. This photo was taken in 1960 at the very end of this type of operation. (TLC Collection)

Cherry River Boom & Lumber Company's well-maintained and good-looking Shay No. 7 in 1956 is stopped in a siding while waiting for another train to pass. Cherry River was one of the biggest loggers in West Virginia, with both geared and rod locomotives in service. It connected with B&O at Richwood. (William E. Warden Photo, TLC Collection)

Opposite Top: Somewhat north of Anjean, Meadow River Lumber Company's Shay No. 5 is in the woods with it log loader positioning logs on the flats. Behind is the giant, complicated, steam-powered Lidgerwood Log Skidder, a steam operated system of wire ropes and pulleys that dragged the logs to the railroad. (John Krause, TLC Collection)

Opposite Bottom: Headed for Bald Knob, Mower Lumber Co. Shay No. 4 is taking flats up the mountain for a load of logs in November 1956. Today tourists are treated to the same uncommon scenery with the same locomotive on the Cass Scenic Railroad's operation. (Phil Ronfor photo, TLC Collection)

The Middle Fork Railroad operated as a common carrier line though its only customer was its owner, the Moore, Keppel Company. It carried coal from the company's mines and lumber from its mill to the B&O connection here at Midvale. Heisler No. 7 has brought down some hoppers, and possibly some flats of lumber out of sight around the curve, to be sent out over the B&O. (John Krause Photo, TLC Collection)

Another Middle Fork Railroad scene has Heisler No. 7 with a B&O Box car in a lumber yard filled with specially cut stakes, made up for some specific purpose. (John Krause Photo, TLC Collection)

A typical moveable logging camp somewhere on the Mower Lumber Company's land is seen here in 1946. Note the tree limbs stuffed into the log flats' pole pockets to hold the logs in place. Loggers lived in the woods in these primitive conditions for long stretches at a time. (TLC Collection)

Meadow River Lumber Company, with its huge facility at Rainelle, was at one time the world's largest hardwood lumber mill. It was one of the few West Virginia logging roads, perhaps the only, that replaced some of its geared steamers with diesels. This photo was made in March 1960. (William E. Warden Photo, TLC Collection)

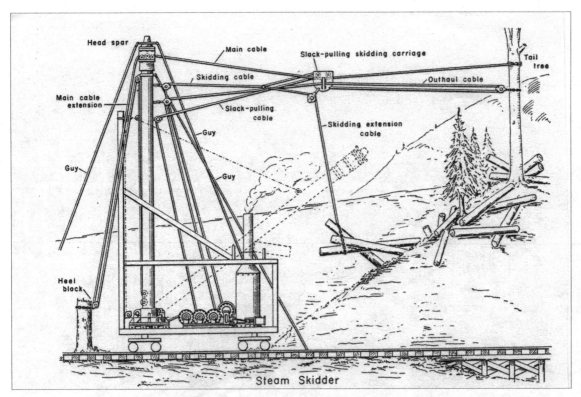

Head spar

Main cable

Slack-pulling skidding carriage

Tail tree

Skidding cable

Main cable extension

Outhaul cable

Slack-pulling cable

Skidding extension cable

Guy

Guy

Guy

Heel block

Steam Skidder

The Lidgerwood steam log skidder was this massive and complicated machine that pulled the logs from the woods down to the railroad where they could be loaded. Introduced in the late 1890s by Lidgerwood Company of New York and first used in West Virginia about 1904, these complicated machines much improved the method of getting logs to the railroad. (TLC Collection)

High on Bald Knob, the boom of the Lidgerwood skidder towers over Mower Lumber Co. log train. The log loader seems to be operating on caterpillar treads instead of the usual tracks that often were laid on the log flats, as it starts to load the logs. (John Killoran Photo)

Made in the USA
Monee, IL
04 June 2024

58891724R00072